Assaulted by Joy

Assaulted by Joy

The Redemption of a Cynic

Stephen W. Simpson

ZONDERVAN®

ZONDERVAN.com/
AUTHORTRACKER
follow your favorite authors

Assaulted by Joy
Copyright © 2008 by Stephen W. Simpson

Requests for information should be addressed to:
Zondervan, Grand Rapids, Michigan 49530

Library of Congress Cataloging-in-Publication Data

Simpson, Stephen, 1969 –
    Assaulted by joy : the redemption of a cynic / Stephen W. Simpson.
      p. cm.
    ISBN 978-0-310-28377-5 (softcover)
     1. Simpson, Stephen, 1969 – 2. Christian biography. I. Title.
  BR1725.S4677A3 2008
  268.092 – dc22   [B]   2008026356

Interior design by Beth Shagene

Printed in the United States of America

08 09 10 11 12 13 14 • 23 22 21 20 19 18 17 16 15 14 13 12 11 10 9 8 7 6 5 4 3 2 1

For Bill

• • •

Contents

Assaulted by Joy

I'M RETURNING FROM A FOUR-MILE RUN AT 8:30 A.M. on a Friday. A chorus of "Dada!" greets me as soon as I open the door. Hayley looks up at my baseball cap and shouts, "Daddy wear funny hat!" and breaks out laughing. A court jester had replaced the docile little girl of only a few months before.

My wife, Shelley, scurries past me, carrying a laundry basket. "Are you ready to take over?" she asks.

"Let me change shirts," I answer. "I'm pretty sweaty."

In confirmation of this, Ella points at my shirt and proclaims, "Daddy all wet. Daddy sticky mess!"

"Right you are, El-Belle," I say, kissing her on the forehead before rushing off to change clothes.

At one year and three months, our quadruplets—yes, I said quadruplets—can walk without falling, but they have yet to develop the speed and agility that will turn them into a roaming toddler hit squad. They are coordinated but not dangerous. Thus, we can care for our children without the assistance of the National Guard (for now). I can even take care of them by myself sometimes, though it isn't easy. At first, I was petrified whenever Shelley left me alone with the kids. I thought that one wrong move would land somebody in the hospital. Now I'm learning that the stakes aren't so high.

I take one-hour shifts before I go to work in the morning. Friday mornings are the best because I get up early and run first. The exercise wakes me up and elevates my mood. That way, the children get to spend time with their father instead of some monstrosity that needs two cans of Red Bull before he can do more than grunt.

I emerge from my bedroom wearing a clean shirt and a fresh coat of deodorant. As soon as I walk through the door, my son Jordan barrels into my legs. He stretches out his arms for me to pick him up. He points to the light switch on the wall and shouts, "Lights!" I hold him up to the switch and he flicks it on and off, laughing with delight. When he's finished, I put him on the ground and he bolts down the hallway like he's running the hundred-yard dash. Jordan regards walking as a poor substitute for sprinting. Since he's built like a cinderblock, it's like having a miniature locomotive in our house.

I walk into the living room and see our daughter Emma sitting in the corner playing with big Lego blocks. I kiss her on the top of her head and she giggles. Then I notice something odd about the Legos. She isn't stacking them like she usually does. When I realize what Emma's doing, I gasp and call Shelley.

My wife darts down the hallway and into the living room with a worried look on her face, because I usually only call her when there's trouble.

"Look what Emma did," I say.

Shelley looks. Then she squeals with delight.

"Emma!" she shouts. "You're so smart! I am so proud of you."

At only fifteen months of age, Emma has arranged the Legos according to size and color. One row has large green blocks. The next has small green blocks. Then there is a row of large red blocks, followed by a small red row, and so on.

Shelley gives Emma a hug, and Emma basks in her mother's affection. Then she picks up the blocks and starts making a tower.

I head to the kitchen to grab a bowl of cereal, but Ella stops me with a large cardboard book in her hands.

"Read book?"

Breakfast can wait.

I sit on the ground, put Ella in my lap, and start reading. Ella repeats everything I say. Then someone accosts me from behind. It's Emma, tickling me and laughing so hard you'd think I was tickling her. No one is safe from a tickling ambush while Emma's around. I let out a desperate laugh until Emma is satisfied that she's subdued her father with mirth. I return my attention to Ella and the book, unaware that Hayley is about to take a nosedive off the couch.

Thud.

I jump up, making sure not to topple Ella, and rush over to Hayley. She's face down on the ground.

"Hayley Rose! Precious, are you okay?"

For a few seconds, she's silent. Then I hear, "Heh, heh, heh, heh …"

I roll her over to find a big, mischievous grin spreading across her face.

"Kaboom!" she shouts.

"You little rascal!" I say and start to tickle her. She rolls around on the floor, laughing.

Hayley's quiet demeanor during her first few months of life was nothing but an act. She was waiting in the wings, observing her audience before she took center stage. She is now a bona fide ham and the biggest comedian in the family. Plus, she knows how to make her father crack up on cue.

The next thing I know, all my children are on me at once. I submit and collapse to the floor on my back. Everyone crawls on top of me, giggling. They are all trying to put their faces on top of mine. I kiss each one of them and they kiss me back, laughing. We frolic around on the floor like this until Shelley walks in.

"Why aren't the kids dressed yet?" she asks.

"Because I've been waylaid by Lilliputians!" I shout. The tired look on Shelley's face disappears as she shakes her head and smiles.

. . .

Sometimes when I look in the mirror, I don't recognize what I see. Where did the angry young man go? Who is this father and husband gazing back at me with crow's feet at the corners of his eyes and thin lines on the edge of his smile? Then I take a second look and realize that I know him, but it's been awhile since we've hung out. He's reemerging from years of cynicism that are being chiseled away by grace.

You see, I'm a jerk. That's the first thing you have to understand. The second thing you have to understand is that you probably are too, sometimes, and we both enjoy it too much. We get a little tickle inside when someone ignores our advice and screws up as a result. We like shutting down people who get in our way and avoiding people who annoy us. We watch Benny Hinn for entertainment value, congratulating ourselves for being too smart to buy what he's selling. We disregard people who don't get our jokes, and we don't suffer fools gladly. We're not evil or even malicious most of the time — just jerks. We have compassion and love, but it doesn't take much for us to roll our eyes and mumble something sarcastic under our breath.

Still, I'm probably more of jerk than you are. It drives me nuts if something interferes with my life. I don't like being bothered, and I don't want any help. If you catch me when I'm in the mood to socialize, you'll love me. Work with my schedule and I'll deliver the sun and the moon. Otherwise, I hate being told what to do, and I have problems with authority. I'm short-tempered when I'm under stress or in a hurry. I start yelling inside my car when another driver cuts me off. As a bonus, I have Attention Deficit Disorder, which means I get impatient, irritated, and bored faster than normal people do.

I am not the guy you'd pick to be the father of quadruplets. But we'll get to that later.

I became a Christian when I was seven years old. I always thought my story would be boring because I met Jesus as a child. Turns out I was wrong. The scary and suspenseful stuff happened after I became a Christian. Sometimes, it happened *because* I was a Christian. In C. S. Lewis's *Surprised by Joy,* his conversion to Christianity comes at the end of the book. The first time I read it, I felt a little cheated by the last page when Lewis realizes, while riding a bus, that he's a Christian. I wanted to know what happened next. I couldn't relate to a story that *ends* with becoming a Christian. In my experience, that's where the story begins.

When I walked down the aisle of a Baptist church as a boy to receive Christ as my Savior, nobody told me that being a Christian is difficult, dangerous even. That information must have been in the fine print. The way I understood it, the closer you were to God, the happier you would be. The less you sinned and the more you followed God's Word, the more your life would be meaningful, happy, and complete. In my years as a follower of Christ, however, I've discovered that the opposite is often true. Don't get me wrong—the most ecstatic, victorious moments of my life resulted from having a relationship with Jesus, but so have the most aggravating and painful ones. Only now am I learning to live in this tension and discover that it can't be any other way.

I think most Christians know this, but we don't like to talk about it because such confessions don't make for the neat, linear success stories that we like to hear. Telling people that being in a relationship with Christ can be maddening and exasperating isn't effective evangelism. You wouldn't put it in a tract or a revival brochure. But I wish someone had told me *at some point*. They didn't have to tell me when I was seven, but they could have clued me in around age fourteen when my theological roof started to cave in. If they had, maybe it wouldn't have taken me decades to figure out that a relationship with God involves a lot of scary twists and turns.

If you've been a Christian for a while, your relationship with God has probably frustrated and frightened you more than once. Maybe you've been confused, angry, or afraid. Maybe nobody told you that was part of the deal when you opened the door of your heart and let Jesus walk in. You also probably didn't realize that some of your brothers and sisters in Christ were going to drive you insane, doing and saying things you find appalling. It's hard to live with all that frustration and confusion when you thought that becoming a Christian guaranteed a life of love and peace.

When I discovered that a relationship with Christ wasn't always warm and fuzzy, I became frightened. Then I got mad. Then I stopped caring. God gave me plenty of opportunities to pursue joy, but cynicism always felt safer. So, instead of offering me joy, he assaulted me with it. When he brought quadruplets to the fight, I had no choice but to shout, "Uncle!" and submit. That's when God made the brown, stagnant rivers in my life flow with golden wine. I drank deep and was born again ... again.

1

Rock and Roll Rebel

"THERE'S NO SUCH THING AS CHRISTIAN ROCK," SAID Brother Jeff. "It's all the devil's music." *Was he throwing out such inanities just to make me crazy? Did he want me to lose my temper so he could kick me out of youth group?*

"How can you say that?" I asked Brother Jeff. "There's nothing about it in the Bible."

My words echoed off the white walls and cardboard ceiling tiles. I could hear the neon lights in the ceiling humming from behind foggy Plexiglas panes. Everyone in the junior high youth group sat in tense silence. Some just stared at the faded green carpet, averting their eyes from the conflict. Others slumped down into the old, overstuffed couches, venturing sheepish glances as they clutched throw pillows. Most of my pubescent peers, however, were on the edge of their seats, transfixed as the forty-year-old associate pastor and I, the fourteen-year-old youth group president, tried to bludgeon each other with words.

"Rock and roll is the music of rebellion," said Brother Jeff. "Even if the lyrics are supposedly Christian, the music makes people lustful and contentious." His mouth was smiling, but his eyes were narrow.

"But it doesn't say that in the Bible!" I shouted. Brother Jeff was wearing me down with edicts that sounded authoritative but made no sense. Every time I presented a reasonable argument, Brother Jeff shot back with something asinine wrapped in a mature, patronizing tone. I was about to pop a blood vessel, and Brother Jeff was as agitated as I was. His face bore a pleasant smile, but the pale, freckled skin beneath his fiery red hair was getting pinker by the second.

"Psalm 98 talks about making all kinds of loud noises before the Lord," I said. "That sounds a lot like Christian rock to me."

"You are perverting God's holy word with that interpretation."

"I absolutely refuse to accept that," I said.

"Then you need to ask God for wisdom," he shot back with an eerie calm. "You need to respect the leaders God has given you. After God, you must respect and obey your parents. After them, you must respect and obey your church authorities. That means me."

Then he turned to the rest of the kids and said, "If you don't believe that rock music makes people rebellious, just look at who's rebelling." Then he laughed. I heard somebody in the back whisper, "Oooh ..." the universal confirmation that you've just received a verbal smackdown.

I gritted my teeth and lurched forward. I might have even growled. One of my friends put a hand on my arm and eased me back in my chair. I had lost this battle, but the war was just beginning.

• • •

I grew up in Lexington, Kentucky. On the surface, Lexington

is about three things: basketball, horses, and shopping centers. Children cut their teeth on the first two. If you meet someone from Lexington who seems shy and reserved, ask about horse racing or University of Kentucky basketball. You'll hear more than you ever wanted about Secretariat and Seattle Slew, including their bloodlines and the farms where they were bred and trained. You'll be informed that Keeneland racetrack is far superior to that tourist slum, Churchill Downs. Want to see a real, live nervous breakdown? Just bring up the game-winning shot by Duke's Christian Laettner in the 1992 East Regional Finals of the NCAA tournament. It halted UK's run to the Final Four and sent the entire state into a coma. That game is the Alamo for Wildcat fans, and no one in the Bluegrass State has ever recovered.

The shopping centers you won't hear about. While I was growing up, Lexington spilled over its borders, swallowing up farms and turning them into parking lots encircled by Wal-Marts, Blockbusters, Payless Shoe Stores, and frozen yogurt stands. Stick an Applebee's in the middle and you've got the building block of Lexington consumerism: the high-fat, middle-class strip mall.

Downtown Lexington, however, stands steadfast amidst the city's suburban sprawl. Stately stone buildings from the early twentieth century line Main Street and Vine in solid indifference to the commercial aspirations of the periphery. The two skyscrapers look like an afterthought, gaudy glass trees in a baroque stone garden. The neighborhoods downtown have housing projects, historic brownstones, and beautiful estates. Artists, ethnic minorities, students, and college professors reside in these, politely ignoring the rest of the city. Attempts to put in chain restaurants or big retail stores usually fail, while small businesses thrive. The best food, the most exotic clothes, and the only art that isn't a painting of a horse or a sketch of a basketball jersey can be found downtown.

The horse farms rest just outside town, where the suburbs surrender to green fields cascading over rolling hills. White and black picket fences create boundaries for the dark, gleaming horses that sustain all this beauty. Majestic barns—more opulent than any house I'll ever own—sit atop hills like castles of feudal kingdoms. Out there, the culture clash between urban and suburban becomes irrelevant. Out there, you just feel lucky to live in Kentucky.

Though I loved the horse farms and found downtown fascinating and alluring, I was a child of the suburbs. I spent my youth running through manicured subdivisions and shopping centers. The suburbs were also the place where big churches popped up like mushrooms. Evangelical Christianity was the second-largest religion in Lexington, right behind basketball. My family attended a mammoth Baptist church that, like many, had moved away from downtown so it could swell and spread on the edge of town. My parents started attending the church because of its large, vital youth program. They wanted my two sisters and me to have a place where we could grow in the love and knowledge of the Lord.

And that's what happened.

When I was seven years old, I began a journey with God that would be the source of more frustration and fear, as well as more joy and wonder than I could imagine. The high school choir had returned from their summer tour to perform a homecoming concert. This was a big deal at my church. The youth choir practiced all year long and toured the country for two weeks every summer. The congregation welcomed them back as conquering heroes, and the homecoming concert was one of the major events of the year. There was always a lot of laughing, crying, and hugging, the climax of which was an invitation to receive Christ that went on for at least thirty minutes. We sang "Just As I Am" ten times in a row, the organist doing her best to mix things up as she reached the seventh chorus. But nobody seemed to mind. People, mostly teenagers (some from the choir, even), flocked down front to accept Jesus as their savior.

Despite all the commotion, I was bored and fidgety. I spent most of the concert drawing pictures on the offering envelopes. I drew everything from spaceships to army men to Batman giving the Joker a much deserved beatdown. But when the invitation began, something happened. I had feelings I didn't understand and couldn't name. Looking back, I'm pretty sure the Holy Spirit was at work. It had to be him, because before the invitation, I was only thinking about when the service would be over. All of a sudden, I felt a strange urge to become closer to God. It wasn't about salvation or avoiding hell—for a reason I can't explain, I wanted to graduate to a higher level of faith. I wanted that relationship with Jesus that I'd heard so much about.

When I told my parents that I wanted to go down front, they looked surprised. They must have wondered why the fidgety kid defacing church bulletins all of a sudden wanted a religious experience. My mother wore a floral dress with a shiny brooch, and my father had on a sport coat but no tie because it was the evening service. Mom looked at me with her trademark sideways gaze beneath raised eyebrows. When she saw I was serious about going down front, she smiled. Dad leaned in close and said, "Do you understand what this means?"

I nodded my head. He put his arm around me and squeezed my shoulder.

"All right, buddy," he said. "Go ahead."

I scurried down front, and the pastor took my small hand in his gigantic one. It was red and warm, like my father's. He asked me if I was certain that I wanted to receive Christ as my Lord and Savior. I told him that I was. He told me to sit up front with one of the deacons until after the service.

After the concert, the pastor took me back to his office. There was shiny wood everywhere and more books than I'd ever seen outside of a library. I sat in a chair that was too big for me, and the pastor sat down across from me, leaning in close.

"Do you understand what it means to commit your life to Christ?" he said, his voice deep and rolling. It felt weird to hear him speaking to me alone instead of to the whole congregation.

"I think so," I said. "It means I become a Christian."

"Yes," said the pastor. "But that means you ask Jesus to forgive you of your sins and come and live inside your heart forever. Are you ready to do that?"

To my seven-year-old brain, having Jesus live inside my heart sounded like just about the coolest thing in the world.

"Yes," I said. "I'm ready to accept Jesus into my heart."

The pastor led me in prayer, asking me to repeat after him. When we were finished, he told me that I was a Christian now. He said that I was going to heaven and that God loved me. It felt like I had joined a special club. When I left the pastor's office, my parents were waiting for me. I started prattling about going to heaven and having Jesus inside my heart. My father said that he was proud. My mother kept asking me what led me to make this decision. Was it the sermon? The music? But I didn't know what to tell her. I just knew that I wanted to become a Christian, and now I was one. I was elated.

We left church and went to Shoney's. My stomach started to growl at first sight of the twenty-foot Big Boy with his wide-eyed smile and red-and-white checkered overalls. I got a burger as big as my hand with cheddar cheese dripping down the side, accompanied by fries that were thick and salty. I cleaned my plate and felt good about it. As I got into bed that night, I felt safe, full, and warm.

For the next seven years, I went to church whenever the doors were open. I loved not only the people, but the building itself. It was big, austere, and mysterious. It contained dozens of secret places—kitchens, alcoves, storage closets, baptismal pools, and large meeting halls. I explored every one of them. The building was almost a metaphor for God—large and strong with endless mysteries to investigate.

I also read the Bible constantly and pestered adults with a million of questions about God. I wanted to be involved in everything. Adults described me as "wise beyond my years" and "a young Bible scholar."

Now, before you start thinking I was a budding young saint, let me explain the other reason I loved church. I didn't have many friends at school. I was fat (I weighed more at age fourteen than I do right now), with buck teeth and the most severe case of acne in the history of Western civilization. Making matters worse, my pituitary gland went off like a hand grenade at age eleven, dragging me into adolescence two years ahead of my peers. I shot up a dozen inches over my friends, but I didn't get any thinner. Instead, my acne got worse and I developed body odor. I started shaving with my dad's electric razor in sixth grade. This produced a red razor burn across my neck that made me look like I'd been hanging from a noose. Oh yeah, and my eyebrows grew together, creating a unibrow.

The prepubescent world did not react kindly to a massive, hairy man-child with skin like a leper. Kids called me fatso, pizza face, lard butt, and the like. I hung around other unpopular kids at school, arguing about who would win in a fight between Luke Skywalker and Superman. The only consolation was that nobody tried to beat me up since I was roughly the size of a duplex.

At church, however, things were different. From the time I was ten until I was sixteen, everything at church revolved around two things: the Bible and singing. By the time I was twelve, I knew more about the Bible than most of the adults at the church. During Sunday school and Bible study, I felt smart and important instead of fat and ugly. When we weren't studying the Bible, we were in choir practice. Our church had a large, active music ministry, and they started asking you to sing not long after you could walk. I'm not Pavarotti or even Barry Manilow, but I sing pretty well. Sometimes I was even asked to fill in for someone in the adult choir if they couldn't make a Sunday morning. I was singing solos by the time I was thirteen. So, between my Bible IQ and my vocal chords, I almost passed for cool at church.

God had granted me a place to escape the pain of the world outside and fall in love with him. Heaven and earth merged as I studied the Bible and spent every spare minute at church. The people at church took care of me. I loved them, we all loved God, and everyone was happy. The solution to life's problems could be found in each other, the Bible, and a God who could do anything and save anybody. Life was perfect, and I believed it would stay that way for eternity.

I was wrong.

. . .

When I was almost fourteen, my parents and I moved to a new house and they ceded the entire basement to me. My sisters, eleven and fourteen years older, had long since moved away, so there was no competition for space. That basement became my escape from the rest of the world, albeit a very loud one.

By eighth grade, I had constructed a massive stereo system. The components were mismatches from different eras of technology. It was an ugly, hulking thing that leaned forward like some aluminum tower of Pisa. But it sounded good. And it was loud. I had four speakers in my den and strung wire under the brown shag carpet to juice up two more in my bedroom. All around the basement, rock and roll spewed forth from trembling woofers behind black mesh screens encased in particleboard.

I had enough music down in that hole to wait out a nuclear winter. When I was a teenager, the digital age was still twenty years away, so I had vinyl albums. Stacks of albums. At seven dollars a pop, my allowance and money from part-time jobs helped me buy four or five records a month. By the time I was sixteen, I had more than two hundred rock albums. Old records, new records, imported records, used records, and bootleg records stood in teetering columns around my basement. I spent hours listening to them while gazing in wonder at the artwork on the sleeves and pouring over the liner notes. Whenever my father told me what a waste of money it all was, I just looked at him like he was out of his mind.

The basement's seclusion from the rest of the house gave me solitude, but the music made it my sanctuary. Music was my elixir, the only other thing than prayer and the Bible that made me feel quiet inside. One night at a party, I saw a girl on whom I had an obsessive crush kissing another guy. I returned home shaking with rage and sadness. But that same night MTV televised a concert that the radio was broadcasting at the same time. This was before every TV in the world offered hi-fi sound, so hearing music from television in stereo over hundred-watt speakers seemed like a miracle. And by a divine stroke, my favorite band was performing: Queen. While not the most morally pure band in the world, their music was amazing. Freddie Mercury pranced around the twenty-inch screen while the speakers hummed to life with the sound of Brian May's guitar. I knew every song by heart and lip-synched the words, dancing around the room in a hypermasculine imitation of Freddie. By the third song, I had forgotten that nasty kiss. When the concert was over, I went to bed and fell into a deep sleep without dreams.

You'd think rock and roll fanaticism wouldn't go over well in a fundamentalist Baptist church, but that wasn't the case. Though our leaders had evangelical fervor, they weren't legalistic. They encouraged us to be obedient to God and were quick to correct us when we got out of line, but they weren't rigid or heavy-handed. Brother Rob was our youth pastor back then, and he was a man of passion and talent. He nurtured everyone's gifts and took an interest in our lives. On a bus ride once,

Brother Rob sat next to me and listened to several Queen songs in a row as I prattled on about the intricacies of the music. He did his best to seem interested, poor guy. He cheered along with everyone else on the bus as I played air guitar during "We Will Rock You," looking like a wooly mammoth having a seizure. Brother Rob and our other leaders were conservative fundamentalists but, as long as God remained top priority, they didn't sweat the small stuff.

They even knew how to disagree with me. They expressed concern about some of the music I listened to, like AC/DC (hard to argue with that one), but they always listened to my perspective. One year, our church went through the inevitable spinning-records-backwards-to-unmask-the-devil phase. I watched in horror as beloved leaders spun records backwards and told us that the resulting gobbledygook said things about worshiping the devil. Though it drove me nuts, it was also one of the most exciting times I had in church because my leaders allowed me to debate them. They let me lead an entire youth meeting providing an alternative perspective on rock and roll and all this back-masking nonsense. They didn't always agree with me, but they respected my right to challenge them. They let me play almost anything I wanted to on summer mission trips as long as the lyrics weren't too sketchy. And I could play Christian rock all day long. The music might sound like someone murdering cats with chainsaws, but as long as the lyrics were about Jesus, they didn't care.

But Brother Jeff cared. He cared a lot.

Brother Jeff became the associate pastor of my church when I was in the eighth grade. In addition to his administrative duties, he was in charge of the youth program. On his first day, the youth and their parents gathered in the gymnasium to meet him.

The senior pastor walked into the gym escorting the thinnest adult male I had ever seen. He had a comical head of curly red, almost orange, hair. His freckles gave the rest of his skin a similar orange glow. He looked like a carrot.

"God bless you," said Jeff the Carrot. "I have been praying for this church, praying that God will guide me and continue his great work with the young people of this congregation." He talked for over an hour in a nasal southern drawl about his vision for the youth program. He told us "God's gonna do this" and "God's gonna do that" and "God's gonna bless y'all." I still knew next to nothing about Jeff except that he looked like a carrot in a red clown wig that talked like it was yanked out of the dirt somewhere in south Georgia. The only relevant thing he told us was that the youth were allowed to call him by his first name. How magnanimous.

The adults asked questions first. "What is your vision for our youth ministry?" "What are your outreach plans?" "What's your philosophy on biblical teachings for teens?" Blah, blah, blah. No one in the room under twenty cared about any of this. The "young people" only cared about one thing. *Could we hang out with this guy? Was he cool?* I don't mean "cool" like hip or even youthful. Nothing is more embarrassing than an old guy trying to act young. We wanted to know if he was someone we could trust. I took it upon myself to find out.

I raised my hand and the senior pastor recognized me.

"What's your favorite Christian rock band?"

Though a silly question, I wanted to give Brother Jeff an easy way to connect with the youth in the room. The question got a few chuckles, which lightened the mood in the room.

But Brother Jeff did anything but laugh or connect with the youth. He breathed a heavy, affected sigh and rolled his eyes toward the heavens.

"Stephen, or is it Stevie?" he asked without waiting for the answer. "I'm afraid you might not care for my answer, which saddens me. But ultimately I answer to God and not to you or any of you other wonderful young people. My answer to your question is this: None. I think Christian rock is an abomination of all the other wonderful music that God has given us. Those rancid, screeching guitars and that horrid pounding beat are, I believe, unleashed from the pit of hell. I despise Christian rock. Secular rock is worse, of course. I will abide none of it on my watch. No form of rock music will be played at any of our activities."

He looked me in the eye and said, "I'm sorry."

My stomach lurched upward as I tried to comprehend what was happening.

Jeff inundated us with a whole new list of prohibitions, ones I had never heard nor imagined despite years of fundamentalist religion: no card playing (a surefire gateway to gambling), no ghost stories (a guaranteed way to conjure demons), no celebration of Halloween (more demons), and no movies unless they were rated "G." He also forbade us to wear shorts, even though our mission trips visited states such as Georgia and Louisiana in the middle of August on a bus with no air conditioning. When I heard that, I could contain myself no longer. Without raising my hand I blurted out, "No shorts on our summer mission trips? The bus has no air conditioning. We'll all melt. And we'll stink!"

That got a lot of laughs, but His Carrotness didn't back down.

"I know it will be uncomfortable. But that's nothing compared to the discomfort Christ experienced dying for our sins. Our mission trips will be the most important time for us to set an example to the pagan world, and we will not be wearing shorts."

A low whistle of amazement came from the back of the gym. Jeff's eyes darted around looking for the culprit before he regained his composure and flashed an ultra-white smile.

No one asked any more questions after that. The senior pastor smiled and said something about us having plenty of time to get to know each other. He said it like it was a good thing.

I thought I was going to puke right on the gym floor. I had fought a long and hard battle for rock and roll at my church and finally gotten my mentors to listen. Now some guy shows up and, with a wave of his hand, banishes all music featuring guitars that plugged in, along with all other benign comforts of the flesh. I was in the middle of a bad dream.

Most teenagers would have stopped coming to youth group or just paid lip service to the new rules and gone about the time-honored practice of rebelling in secret. Not me. I declared war. This was *my* church. Church was the only place where I felt safe, understood, and respected. It was the only place I had fun. Now some dogmatic cleric was trying to ruin it for me. *Over my dead body.*

Poor Brother Jeff had no idea who he was up against. In a Southern Baptist Church, the Bible is the litmus test for everything. Ever since I'd walked down the aisle at age seven and taken the pastor's hand, I'd been reading the Bible. I didn't just listen to what my teachers told me about the Bible in Sunday school; I studied the thing. By age thirteen, I'd read the entire Bible (well, almost—I got the K.O. from Numbers in chapter 3). I knew that biblical support for Brother Jeff's list of "don'ts" was thin at best, and I wielded the Word like a sword in our theological debates. I was certain that my knowledge of Scripture would help me triumph over this new regime of the absurd.

I debated Jeff steadily for the next year, always using what I regarded as solid biblical arguments. I prayed for him and for our church. I did my best to be a good example and a solid leader so that my disagreements with Jeff didn't look like reckless defiance. I tangled with Jeff in public, in private, and in writing. I fought my war with prayerful diligence and refused to back down. For a long time, I thought I was winning. There was no way that this man could continue imposing ridiculous rules that were biblically unsound, not to mention wildly unpopular.

Well, at least they were unpopular at first ...

One day I was talking to another guy in the youth group I liked and respected. He was a couple of years older, and I'd always considered him cool. He had introduced me to Christian rock, telling me about bands like Petra and Servant. We went to Christian rock concerts together and danced and sang and went bananas in the name of the Lord.

One day I commiserated with him, "It's not right that Brother Jeff won't let us listen to Christian rock."

"There's no such thing as Christian rock," he said with a blank expression. "It's all of the devil." He didn't elaborate, just looked at me with mute finality. I didn't say anything because, in that moment, I realized that there was nothing to say. It didn't matter if I was right or wrong about rock music, wearing shorts, playing cards, or whether the earth was round or flat. My friend's mind was made up. The validity of my arguments was irrelevant. Brother Jeff had given an edict, and my friend accepted it without question.

For the first time in my life, I felt nervous and alone at church. That might not have been so bad if I didn't feel nervous and alone everyplace else.

. . .

On the first day of school in ninth grade, a cute girl called me "Piggy" without provocation. I gave her a dirty look, but that night I lay in bed crying. Jeff had invaded my last safe haven, abandoning me to a place where pretty girls likened me to swine. Life couldn't continue like this. Drastic times called for drastic measures.

First, I started taking the medication Accutane, a drug that eliminates acne with the gentleness of atomic radiation. I endured nausea, headaches, nosebleeds, and wisps of hair falling out until the medication ran its course and my face no longer resembled a map of the Himalayas. Next, I lost weight. I dropped fifty pounds in six months. Despite my girth, I'd always been strong and athletic. I could outrun kids half my size, and I could bench press two hundred pounds by age fourteen. I lost weight mainly through running long distances and cutting out sweets. As a result, I lost more fat than I did muscle. By the last day of ninth grade, I had changed from an acne-covered behemoth into a lean, muscular jock with unblemished skin.

That summer, I went to a Christian camp with one of my

friends from church named Gordon Green. Gordy was a stud. He was good-looking, smooth, and had no trouble with the ladies. On our first night at camp, Gordon spotted a brunette he found attractive. He dispatched one of our female friends to inform the young lady of his affections and ascertain her level of interest in him. Ten minutes later, our friend returned with the verdict.

"So, does she like me?"

"She says that you're cute," the emissary replied as a Casanova grin spread across Gordon's face.

"But she thinks Steve is cuter."

Gordon was speechless; I was thunderstruck.

"Could you repeat that?" I said, partly because I wanted to make sure I heard her right, but mostly because I just wanted to hear it again.

Despite the nice ego boost, I entered high school in the fall with my head down. I looked different, but I still didn't have many friends. The first day of high school is hard for anyone, but going through it alone is anxious drudgery. I zipped through the hallways avoiding eye contact with everyone. On my way to second period, someone grabbed my shoulder and spun me around.

"Lookin' good, Simpson. Looks like you'll be ready to wrestle this year," said Mac Wood, a senior on the wrestling team with me. That was the first time he'd said anything nice to me.

"Thanks," I said, wondering if I was supposed to say something cocky or funny instead.

"See you in practice," he said and disappeared.

In third-period Biology, a popular member of the football team took a seat next to me.

At lunch I sat down alone, but my friend Bill asked me to sit with him and four of his friends who'd never talked to me before. Later that week, we all played basketball at Bill's house. By Christmas, we were sitting together on the bus. By springtime, we were hanging out over the weekend.

It was surreal. I figured that losing pounds and zits would make things easier. I didn't know that it would make me need church a whole lot less.

· · ·

In March of my tenth-grade year, I told my mother that I didn't want to go to youth group anymore. She said that she didn't care; I was going anyway.

"You don't forsake the body of Christ just because you don't like one of its parts. Is Jesus still the most important thing in your life?"

"Yes, Mom," I said, rolling my eyes.

"Following him isn't always easy. Sometimes we have to show Christ's love to people we don't like."

I knew she was right, but I didn't like it. My father's take on the situation made sticking with church a little easier.

"If you think Brother Jeff is wrong, you need to stick to your guns. If you leave youth group, that means he wins. You've let him chase you off. Stick around and stand up for what you believe.

Now that I could do, though perhaps not in the way Dad imagined.

That summer, I went on the youth mission trip as I had every year. Since Brother Jeff wouldn't let us wear shorts, I boarded the bus wearing mesh, see-through sweatpants over my shorts, obeying the letter of the law while gleefully defying the spirit. When Jeff saw me, he just shook his head, frustrated but impotent because I'd conformed to his rules. I whispered ghost stories to the other kids just because it wasn't allowed. I organized card games at the back of the bus. Whenever Brother Jeff wandered back, we'd chuck the Jacks and Queens, whip out a deck of Uno, and beam at him like little cherubs. But the real *coup d'etat* was smuggling rock and roll onto the bus.

I stuffed a bunch of socks with cassette tapes and hid them in the bottom of my luggage. Thus, the 1985 youth mission trip rolled out of town carrying every album by Queen and U2, along with a strong sampling of The Who, The Clash, Rush, Van Halen, and anything else that sounded like something Brother Jeff would hate. My buddy Gordon was the only person I told about it, which turned out to be a big mistake.

After eating lunch at a Cracker Barrel, we got back on the bus and discovered Gordon sitting in my seat holding my boom box. Ozzy Osbourne's "Revelation (Mother Earth)" blasted out of the speakers at about five thousand decibels. One of the adult volunteers told Gordon to turn it off. Gordon protested, saying that he thought the music sounded awesome. I shot Gordon a look that said, "I am going to kill you with my bare hands." He turned the music off and apologized. Gordon didn't rat me out, but he didn't have to. It wasn't hard for anyone to figure out who snuck Ozzy on the bus.

When Brother Jeff found out, he gave me a look of contempt ... and nothing more. I expected dire consequences, confiscation of my tapes at the minimum. But he didn't do anything.

The next day, we had three hours to wander around Jefferson

City, Missouri. The place was filled with novelty shops, theme restaurants, and other attractions that teenagers live for. They also happened to have a palm reader, which piqued my interest.

At a Cub Scout Halloween party in second grade, somebody's mom had dressed up like a gypsy and read our palms. The whole thing was a joke, but the palm reader said something that stuck with me. She said I was going to marry a girl named Jenny. It just so happened that I'd had a crush on a girl named Jenny since seventh grade. Jenny was with me that day in Jefferson City as we passed a palm reader's hut adorned with flashing astrological symbols.

I had told Jenny about the palm reader back when I'd been fat and ugly. That was when she'd told me she liked me "as a friend," the label that every adolescent suitor regards as a curse. But things were different now. Jenny had been flirting with me lately. Maybe it was time to reintroduce the subject.

"Hey, Jenny, remember the story I told you about that palm reader saying I would marry a girl named Jenny?" I said, pointing to the palm reader's hut.

Jenny flashed a feline grin and said, "I remember. Maybe you should get a second opinion."

I needed nothing more. Without a second thought, I ducked into the palm reader's lair.

Five minutes later and five dollars poorer, I had no new information regarding the name of my bride-to-be. (For the record, my wife's name is not Jenny and her parents never even considered that name.) I laughed it off as confirmation that palm reading was a bunch of hooey.

Since I have a big mouth, I told half a dozen people about

the palm reader. Someone tattled. At our next stop, Brother Jeff and one of the volunteers cornered me. They took me into the sanctuary of the church that was putting us up for the night. Brother Jeff suggested we sit in the choir loft. It felt like being in the penalty box at a hockey game.

"Steve, the fact that you went to a palm reader grieves me, but I hate to say that I'm not surprised," began Brother Jeff as the volunteer frowned and nodded in agreement. "I have sensed this sort of lawlessness in you from the first time we met almost three years ago. In those three years, things seem to have only gotten worse. What on earth gave you the notion of going to a palm reader?"

I told him the story about the gypsy at Cub Scouts and Jenny. I didn't want to, but I thought Jeff would cut me some slack if I humiliated myself.

Jeff furrowed his brow and nodded.

"It's all starting to make sense now. If you went to a palm reader in Cub Scouts, that would have opened you to demonic influence at a vulnerable age. That's probably the reason you're so obsessed with rock music. It explains your contentious nature."

That just made me mad. I forgot about trying to get out of this unscathed.

"I told you that the palm reader at Cub Scouts was just a joke. I went to the palm reader today just as a stunt to impress Jenny. I promise you, Jeff, no demons were involved."

"The Prince of Lies wants you to think that."

I rolled my eyes. Bad move.

"You might not care about your own spiritual welfare, but I care about this youth group. You have opened the whole youth group to demonic oppression through this act. We have to intervene with prayer."

So far Jeff had said nothing about calling my parents or sending me home. My worst fear was that he would make my parents come and take me home. This would result in nothing less than being thrown in a dungeon and forced to eat spiders until I was forty-five. So when Jeff told me that all he wanted to do is pray, my insides broke into applause. I let prudence prevail.

"Okay," I said. "Let's pray."

We bowed our heads. Jeff and the volunteer were silent for a few seconds. Nobody spoke in tongues in our church, but they made a lot of other noises. Jeff started doing that humming thing, going, "Hmm ... yes, Lord ..." When Jeff finally started to form complete sentences, I thought it might have been better to be sent home.

"Demon of divination, demon of rebellion, demon of contentiousness ..."

Was he talking to me? I hoped that he was just using hyperbole and not—

"We cast you out of Stephen in the name of the Father, the Son, and the Holy Ghost and by the power of the blood of the Lamb."

Oh. No. He. Didn't.

"Dear Jesus, we ask that, through the power of your precious blood, you release Stephen from demonic oppression and set him upon a righteous path. Bring him back into your glorious light and renew his heart and mind. Please build a hedge around this youth group. Send your angels to protect us from any demonic influence that this palm reader may have introduced."

The volunteer said "Hmmm ..." so many times that he

sounded like a bathroom fan. I was trying not to scream, "Are you out of your mind?" at the top of my lungs. But since I didn't want to get pinned to the floor and doused with holy water, I started saying my own silent prayer instead.

This is stupid, Lord. You know that I don't have any demons inside me. I'm sorry for doing something wrong to impress a girl. I thought of it as a joke, but I should have been more serious. Demons? You gotta be kidding me! I'll tell you what, God. If I really am under demonic influence, make that clear to me right now. Give me a sign, and I'll go with this. I ask it in Jesus' name.

I felt nothing. No physical, spiritual, or emotional signs that I was possessed. I felt convicted over committing a sin. I even felt bad about upsetting Brother Jeff. Other than that, nothing. I stopped praying and returned my attention to Jeff, who was still casting out demons.

Something started to freeze inside me. My anger drained away, replaced by cool apathy. I no longer wanted to debate Jeff. I didn't even want to rebel against him. The absurdity of what was happening was too much. There was no way to change Jeff's mind. The only sensible thing to do was stop caring.

◆ ◆ ◆

In that moment, a cynic was born. But it was not Brother Jeff's fault. It was mine.

I chose to handle my anger and pain by killing off the passion that created it. I had my nice, safe little Christian world, and I threw a fit when someone changed things. I couldn't handle it when I didn't get my way. I couldn't accept the fact that things weren't perfect anymore, so I made Brother Jeff the enemy. For years, well into adulthood, I imagined Brother Jeff as an evil despot who stomped on a vibrant faith with legalistic oppression. That's what cynicism does—it splits the truth in half. In your preoccupation with the things that hurt you, you forget the things that nurtured you.

Cynicism begins as passion. This is especially true for Christians who fall in love with Jesus when they're young. We give our lives to something beautiful and pure, believing that it will never be tarnished. We embrace our church and the warmth and love of its people. We experience spiritual highs that set us ablaze with fervor for Christ. We want to tell other people in hopes that they will discover this same joy. We pray, study the Bible, and become enraptured by our relationship with God and his church. For a little while, it's like walking in Eden with God.

Then a serpent shows up and tells us about a fruit that will make us smarter. In a moment of selfishness and fear, we take a bite. Everything changes. We see that the leaders we idealize are flawed and broken. We look around the garden and see hypocrisy and deceit. We see people twisting our beloved Scripture to bully people who disagree with them. People we love and trust hurt us, sometimes through malice, but more often weakness. Our peaceful, perfect garden becomes a forest filled with monsters, and we flee.

Beneath the surly and sarcastic exterior of a cynic lies a broken heart. Most cynics once believed in something with all their hearts and minds. Then something caused pain and disappointment. It was so terrible that we vow never to let it happen again. We stop trusting. We suspect anyone who proclaims simple truths. We think that pat answers are for suckers, because we've been the sucker before. So we stop going to church or, if we do go, we don't get involved. We don't just question religious authority; we mock it. We refuse to be vulnerable and embrace the love we once knew because we're terrified that it will leave us again.

Oscar Wilde wrote, "A cynic is someone who knows the price of everything and the value of nothing." Cynics can tell you all about the painful cost of religion, but they no longer know the joy of depending on God and others. After I became a cynic, I still longed for the passion I once felt, but I refused to be fooled again. I refused to be hurt again.

The story about Brother Jeff is one-sided. I told the truth, but it was the cynical truth. I didn't lie, but I didn't tell you the whole story. I left out something really important, because it's painful to think about: Brother Jeff loved me.

For years I imagined that our former leader, Brother Rob, was the one who really cared for me. That's not true. Brother Rob was great, but Jeff nurtured me more. Yes, we fought a lot, but Jeff took an incredible interest in my life. He was legalistic and stubborn, but there is no question that he cared about me. We didn't always argue. We would talk about God, the Bible, or just chew the fat about topics that didn't lead to an argument. Even when were fighting, Jeff invested time and energy in my life. The guy spent hours of his personal time debating a pimple-faced punk about music.

The guy was also a Bible scholar. He taught us things about early Christian history, Greek, and Hebrew that helped me see the Bible in a whole new light. He could give rousing, sincere sermons that inspired and convicted. Despite my anger at Brother

Jeff's rules, my knowledge and love of the Lord grew under his leadership.

And the guy was funny. He was a great practical joker with a lightning-fast wit. He was open and gregarious most of the time. He even made fun of his appearance, saying that his red hair and freckled skin made him look like a reject from the Partridge Family. He could be cocky, but he could also show humility and confess his sins. For years, I didn't allow myself to remember that. The cynic could never admit that his enemy was so friendly and so much fun. I was too busy judging him.

In other words, I was too busy sinning against him.

I stopped going to youth group after the palm-reading/exorcism incident. I still attended Sunday morning services because my mother would have shaved her head otherwise. Then, in the spring of my junior year, I visited the Methodist church down the road because a cute girl invited me. The youth group was almost identical to my old one—active, passionately evangelical, big choir, summer trips—except for Jeff's rules. I got to listen to all the rock and roll I wanted, wear shorts, play cards, and nobody tried to pluck any demons out of me.

My parents were understandably disappointed that I was attending a different church than they were, but I think they understood. They knew that my faith was important to me and supported my search for a place where I could worship in peace.

My new youth pastor, Allen, was a wise and gentle mentor. He got past my suspicions, helped me assimilate into my new group, and became a trusted friend. He was exactly the kind of tender, listening leader that I needed to help me recover from the pain of losing the church of my childhood.

But I hadn't heard the last of Brother Jeff. The summer between my junior and senior year, I got a letter from him, though I hadn't seen him in months. In the letter, Brother Jeff asked me to return to youth group. His words bore no condemnation or judgment. He just said that things weren't the same without me, and he wanted me to come back. He invited me to go on the summer mission trip. He wrote, "Just call me up and say, 'Jeff, I'm going.' You don't have to say anything more than that and you'll be welcome to come. Otherwise, who's going to ask the tough questions? Who's going to keep me in line?"

Who's going to keep me in line? This maniac was inviting the very thing that I thought he hated about me?

Jeff, I'm going. That's all I have to say? After so much strife, three words will set things right again?

Despite Jeff's vulnerability and courage, his words rolled off me. I didn't believe him. I couldn't tolerate the idea that I was important to him. I couldn't believe that I'd impacted his life. He drove me crazy, but he cared enough about me that I drove him crazy too. That's the danger of passion. The things we love, the things that bring us the most joy, make us crazy. Whether it's God, a person, a church, or a cause, to love something is to sacrifice peace. The world and all the people in it are broken. Love cannot exist without pain. I think this is what Jesus meant when he said, "I did not come to bring peace, but a sword" (Matthew 10:34). I doubt that he was warmongering or undercutting pacifism. Maybe he meant that giving your life to something results in strife. You cannot have passion for something and be free from pain.

This was a lesson I would not learn for a very long time. I'm still not sure I get it. God's tried to teach me again and again, but I have difficulty accepting it. I've got to get used to it, though, because the other option is despair. It's the way of the cynic, who sneers and makes a stone of his heart because passion is too dangerous. Being a Christian is supposed to be dangerous. It means being vulnerable, taking risks, and having communities of imperfect people. It means leaving our comfort zone and kissing it good-bye forever. Being a Christian means exchanging comfort for something so much better: joy. Comfort is nothing more than a lack of pain and aggravation. It's about what isn't there instead of what is. Joy comes from passion, love, and commitment to something and Someone bigger than you. Passion, love, and commitment come at a price (just ask Jesus), but it's a price worth paying, because God's joy provides a sense of meaning and a depth of feeling you can't get any other way.

I never wrote Jeff back, and I never saw him again. Caring was too difficult, so I stopped. I wasn't willing to walk the dangerous path that leads to joy.

2

The Church
of Friendship

"WHAT ARE WE DOING THIS WEEKEND?" EDDIE ASKED AS he jumped up and down on the trampoline. It was spring of my sophomore year of high school. The air was crisp but not cold. Wind rustled through trees showing the first sign of green. Eddie and I were bouncing on a trampoline in our neighbor's backyard that was community property, especially when they weren't home.

I was sure I didn't hear him right. He must have said, "What are *you* doing?"

I didn't respond right away because I wasn't sure what to do. I tried to do a back flip and ended up landing on my butt. Eddie laughed and did a back flip effortlessly.

"I haven't really thought about what *I'm* gonna do this weekend," I said, emphasizing the "I'm" part.

"No," said Eddie. "What are *we* doing this weekend?"

The way he asked the question hinted at what we both knew. Eddie and I didn't really hang out beyond riding the same bus home from school and bouncing on this trampoline. We were in some clubs and classes together, but he'd never invited me to do anything with him. Eddie had a lot of friends. I didn't.

So when Eddie asked what "we" were doing that weekend, a turning point arrived.

We moved into Ed's neighborhood when I was fourteen. My sister Suzanne was twenty-five with a place of her own, and my sister Lisa was twenty-eight, married, and living in Virginia. My parents were approaching their sixties and wanted a smaller house in a quieter neighborhood. They also said they wanted to move someplace near "more boys your age." What they didn't know is that all the "boys" in this neighborhood were great friends with each other and not friends with me at all. Eddie asking me to hang out with him was a sign that, after two years, that was starting to change.

I had entered high school adrift. Church was no longer a secure home base. I had a few friends at school, but nothing that resembled the stable community I'd had at church. I didn't have the social currency at school that I once had at church. Since I didn't drink, swear, or talk about sex all the time, I wasn't much of crowd pleaser with the guys. And all I had to do was look around me to see that I didn't know how to dress either. In the mid-eighties hip guys donned mullets (yes, they were cool once), stonewashed denim, and Polo shirts. My mom had a thing for buying jeans that looked like roof shingles and cheap knockoffs of fashionable clothes. Though I didn't look like a total dork, I sure didn't look cool. The only thing going for me was that I wasn't fat and covered with zits anymore. Even that caused some problems. I didn't know who I was in my new body yet, and my peers didn't know what to do with the new Steve either.

Since the beginning of tenth grade, Eddie and the other guys in the neighborhood had been including me more, little by little. Kevin and Sulli were the popular soccer players who shared my love for rock and roll. Patrick was the wild man who frightened and fascinated me at the same time. Stan, my next-door neighbor, was quiet and smart but seemed to be friends with everybody in school. John was the class clown and budding rock musician with a classic '62, baby blue Oldsmobile convertible. That car was so cool it should have been illegal for a sixteen-year-old boy. Every weekend, the guys would ride around all night in John's car. Sometimes they invited me, but I was acutely aware of the many times they didn't.

This time, however, Eddie was making sure that I'd be coming along. We didn't talk about what we were doing, just that we would be doing something. It made me feel relaxed for the rest of the week.

Come Friday night, we still didn't have definite plans. Eddie just said to come over to his house around eight o'clock. He said seven other people would be venturing out with us, so I needed to bring my car. Our friend John would be the other driver, since we were the only ones with driver's licenses.

The fact that John was driving meant that my car would be everyone's second choice for transportation because his car was so rad. I, on the other hand, would be driving my mother's decade-old Caprice Classic. It was a white monstrosity of a car, but it had an eight-cylinder engine with 350 horsepower. I slapped a "God Rules!" bumper sticker on the rear fender and raced around town as fast as my conscience allowed. The guys thought it was hysterical and nicknamed my car "the Godrulesmobile."

I showed up ten minutes late to Ed's house because I didn't want to seem overeager. Stan, my next-door neighbor, was already there.

"Steve!" he exclaimed when I walked into Ed's basement.

Stan was mild-mannered but always seemed glad to see me. He started asking me questions about school, wrestling, a girl he'd heard I had crush on. He was one of the only teenage guys I knew who spent more time asking about other people's lives instead of bragging about his own. I was glad he was the first one there. It helped me calm down.

After a few minutes, Kevin and Sulli showed up together, as always. They were soccer players, which qualified them as studs at my school. I was on the wrestling team, which qualified me as weird in a city obsessed with basketball. Nevertheless, Kevin, Sulli, and I soon fell into conversation about our common passion.

"Sammy Hagar is replacing David Lee Roth as lead singer of Van Halen," Kevin said. "They're going to be awesome."

"He's a better musician," Sulli said. "The songs will rock more."

"And Sammy doesn't have an ego the size of Florida," I added. "That should help."

Kevin and Sulli laughed. I started to feel cool. Then John pulled up in his smooth-mobile. Everyone piled in, leaving me standing alone on the curb. I didn't feel so cool anymore.

"Go get Bill, Patrick, Becky, and Kristin and meet us at Ecton Park," Eddie shouted from the backseat of John's car.

These orders cheered me up. John's car might have been cooler and its occupants more popular, but my car was going to be more fun.

I went to pick up Bill first, looking forward to it the whole way. Bill was the only guy in the group who'd been my friend since junior high. I could talk to Bill about anything, and he would listen with sincere interest. If I found a new band I liked,

Bill wanted to listen to the album with me. If I was having girl problems, Bill was ready to listen and come up with a plan of action, which usually included intercession on his part. And I could talk to Bill about sports for hours. I'd never met another guy who made me feel so comfortable exposing my ignorance about sports trivia. One summer, I went with him to a Reds game and asked him to tell me about the team. By the time Bill was finished, I was an expert on the Cincinnati Reds.

I pulled up in front of Bill's house and honked my horn. Bill's father peered out the window with an annoyed look. Guess I should have gotten out and knocked. The front door opened and Bill bounded out, smiling.

"Steve!" he said. "I didn't know the Godrulesmobile was in action tonight. Are we going to be in a demolition derby against Beelzebub or something?"

"If there was, you know that the Godrulesmobile would crush him," I said. "I think Beelzebub drives a Pinto."

We laughed. I had shared the gospel with Bill so many times that joking about my religion was part of our rapport. He expressed more interest in my faith than any of my non-church friends. The subject was not a sensitive one between us, and we could joke about it.

"I thought you were grounded," I said.

"I talked them out of it," he said. "When I told them you would be coming out with us tonight, they chilled out. They know you don't drink, so they think that means nobody else will."

Bill always threw parties when his parents were out of town. He always got caught and he always got grounded and he always talked them into letting him out of it early. Bill had that kind of charm.

"You going to be okay, tonight?" Bill asked out of nowhere.

"Of course," I said. "Why wouldn't I be?"

"People can get kind of rowdy," he said. "I know you're against drinking and sex—"

"Before marriage," I corrected him. "It's not like I think sex is a bad thing."

"Anyway, I just don't want you to get nervous if we end up at a party. If you start feeling weird, just come hang out with me or something."

"I appreciate it," I said. "But I'll be okay."

Next, we went to Kristin's house to pick up her and Becky. I was on the school newspaper staff with Kristin and Becky. Since we never did any work in that class until a couple weeks before deadline, the three of us spent hours talking. They were the closest female friends I'd ever had. They were cute and funny, and it felt like I was getting away with something when I hung out with them.

Becky and Kristin hopped in the back seat, filling the car with pleasant feminine smells. They were loud and giggly and wonderful. The three of us started goofing around, filling the car with laughter before I'd left Kristin's street. I put in a mix tape and R.E.M.'s "South Central Rain" filled the car. Becky and Kristin teased me about a girl I had a crush on. I pretended to be annoyed even though I enjoyed the attention. I drove along in bliss.

But then we had to pick up Patrick.

He was waiting on the curb in front of his house. He wrinkled his nose when I pulled up.

"How did I end up riding with you instead of John?" he asked.

I said nothing, torn between anger and shame. Kristin rolled down her window and stuck her head out.

"Stop being a jerk, shut up, and get in," she said.

Pat rolled his eyes. "I was just kidding! You know I love riding in the Godrulesmobile. No way we're getting hit by a drunk driver in this thing. Steve's got divine protection."

"We're having a demolition derby with Satan later," Bill announced.

"I thought it was Beelzebub," I said.

"Is there a difference?" asked Bill.

"Yes. Actually—"

"Please, don't get him started," Patrick said.

"Shut up," said Becky. "I want to hear this."

"Me too," said Bill.

I grinned and explained the dark side of the spiritual hierarchy, describing what the Bible had to say before distinguishing it from Dante's version.

When I was finished, Patrick said, "Okay, I admit that was pretty cool. Steve, I'm gonna have to let you explain all this God stuff to me someday. Just not tonight."

Though I never would have told him, I was in awe of Patrick. It wasn't just that he was popular and good-looking; he was bold in ways that I could never imagine. Patrick always said exactly what he thought. He was the most authentic person I'd ever known, in or out of church. It got him into trouble sometimes, but it also drew people to him. I didn't have enough self-esteem to be comfortable around that kind of confidence.

We met up with the others at Ecton Park. To my relief, there was no beer in sight. I didn't mind explaining, once again, why I didn't drink. In fact, it gave me an opportunity to share my faith. But I wasn't in the mood to play missionary tonight. I just wanted to be with friends.

Eddie told us that were going to his new girlfriend's house. Her divorced mother was out on a date, so we would have the place to ourselves. We piled into the cars, the same passengers riding in each, and headed to our new destination.

Once we arrived, Patrick decided that we should play "Truth or Dare" in order to make something interesting happen. We'd only been playing for about five minutes, with no one having taken the "dare" option yet, when we heard a key in the door. Eddie's girlfriend's mom was home two hours early. Ed's girlfriend wasn't allowed to have friends over, so she screamed for everyone to hide. We dashed into the backyard. The fence was too high to climb, and we couldn't escape out the front without being seen. Patrick grabbed a stepladder leaning against a shed and threw it against the side of the house.

"Everybody up!" he said.

We scattered up the ladder and lay flat on the roof. Inside, Ed's girlfriend's mom heard what must have sounded like an avalanche.

She ran out to the backyard and shouted, "Who's on my roof? Come down before I call the police!"

Patrick's response became legendary.

"Nobody up here but us shingles!" he said.

I started laughing so hard that tears came out my eyes, and I couldn't breathe. Sulli's fit of mirth sent him rolling off the one-story roof, and he twisted his ankle. This presented enough of an emergency for Ed's girlfriend's mom to let us leave without interrogation or punishment. We hightailed it out of there, cracking up the whole way home.

• • •

At first, just having a group of friends again was a relief. I had things to do on weekends instead of driving around by myself. Over time, however, my relationship with the guys and Kristin and Becky became something more. As high school went on, we started spending more and more time together. We went to parties (with me, the teetotaling Christian, as permanent designated driver), toilet papered houses, played basketball, chased girls, and did all the other things that are the ethereal bliss of male adolescence. We had experiences that became legend, part of the oral tradition of the tribe. Mostly, however, we were just next to each other all through high school. We'd hang around each other's houses talking, eating, listening to music, or watching television until our parents demanded our return. My friends made me feel settled and quiet inside. They quietly built my self-esteem and confidence. We didn't sit around having deep conversations. We didn't "process" our relationships. We just accepted each other. Eventually, we came to love each other. My friends in high school offered me sanctuary from the storms of adolescence.

They became my church.

As I went through high school, the importance of church diminished in my life. I went to my new church Sunday mornings and stayed active in my new youth group, but it didn't feel like home the way church once had. God was probably sad that church wasn't as important to me, but I also think he understood what I was going through. Maybe that's why he provided Kevin, Sulli, Eddie, Stan, Patrick, John, Becky, and Kristin. I don't think he meant for them to replace church in my life.

Maybe he just wanted to remind me about the joy of friendship. First John 4:12 says, "No one has ever seen God; but if we love one another, God lives in us and his love is made complete in us." My friends may not have been born-again Christians in the legalistic sense, but God lived in our friendships anyway. God wanted me to keep experiencing him. He saw that my growing cynicism about religion was getting in the way of that at church, so he came in through another door. He kept touching me through my friends, reminding me that I still needed other people.

. . .

The night before we all left for college, we gathered at an older friend's apartment for a prolonged, maudlin farewell. Everyone was drinking but me. The more everyone drank, the more everyone cried. But I couldn't blame my tears on anything but sadness. Everything was about to change. Most of us were going to different colleges in different cities. We wouldn't be next to each other every day, lounging on each other's basement sofas, raiding each other's refrigerators, passing notes in class, and yammering about nothing on the phone for hours. It felt like part of me was dying.

I pulled everyone aside, one by one, to say good-bye. I told each what he or she meant to me and thanked them for being in my life. Each conversation ended with long, tearful hugs. The girls kissed me on the cheek, and the guys gave me hard, masculine pats on the back. By the end of the night, we collapsed together on the floor, lying all over each other. People started to trickle away after midnight. Every time someone left, another

round of bawling began. I was one of the last to go, and everyone piled on, soaking my clothes with tears. Patrick tried to
make a joke through a river of snot and tears. Bill threatened
to harm my mother if I didn't write him once a month. Becky
and Kristin grabbed me tight and ruined one of my shirts with
mascara. I felt more love than I ever had in one moment.

Driving home, I cried so hard that it made driving dangerous. The next morning, I got up at six to begin the long drive
to Wake Forest University in North Carolina. I headed east in a
daze, convinced that the best friendships I'd ever had were over.

* * *

In the photograph, I'm surrounded by liquor bottles. I'm lying
on the floor with my eyes closed and my arms draped across
my chest. It looks like I'm dead from too much drinking. Eddie
thought this was particularly funny since, well into my freshman year of college, I still didn't drink a drop.

I had visited him at Clemson for a weekend. We stayed up
all night playing pranks on people in Eddie's dorm. After the
Wake Forest–Clemson football game, I took a nap on the floor
of Eddie's room. Eddie thought it would be funny to make it
look like I passed out after drinking. He said he was going to
save the photo in case he ever needed to blackmail me. As far as
I know, he still has it.

* * *

It's 3:00 a.m. and I can't stop laughing, even though about a
dozen Waffle House patrons are glaring at me. Bill is talking like

Louis Armstrong with straws in his nose. Patrick starts licking grease off the bare countertop. We're on a trip to Myrtle Beach, South Carolina, during the summer between our freshman and sophomore years of college. We've all been saving money from our summer jobs for this vacation, and we're just a little too giddy about being on our own in the middle of nowhere at three o'clock in the morning.

The waitress comes over and says, "You boys need to settle down or I'll have to ask you to leave."

Still imitating Louis Armstrong, Bill says, "Why certainly, my dear." We explode with laughter. We decided to leave right before they kick us out.

. . .

Bill and I both worked together for the city recreation department for two summers. We were both DJ's for our college radio stations, and we conferred at least once a semester to swap ideas.

All through college, Eddie and Kevin had a habit of calling me in the middle of the night, especially if they had been to a party earlier in the evening.

Stan called a lot too, but he did it sober.

Becky and Kristin wrote me letters almost once a week my freshman year and kept it up once a semester after that. Becky even wrote me when I spent a semester in London.

Patrick and I went on several double dates together on summer breaks during college. For some reason, the girls were always annoyed by the end of the evening. Maybe it had something to do with Patrick and me cracking each other up the whole time.

We weren't as close during college as we were in high school.

We were closer.

Though I didn't know it at the time, God was using these friends to teach me about joy. I was preoccupied during high school and college. Grades, wrestling, earning money, and, most of all, finding a girlfriend took most of my time and energy. I was always chasing something, but I always felt at peace around my friends. I was learning about the grounded nature of joy. It's not something to pursue. Usually, God has already given it to you and you just need to pay more attention. Western culture, in particular, is preoccupied with the idea of more—more money, more success, more beauty, more security, more bliss. We spend our lives chasing things that we think will make us complete. Most of the time, God has already surrounded us with things that will give us joy.

I got good grades in college. I had a steady girlfriend. I joined a fraternity and had a busy social life. I even got into the competitive overseas program and spent a semester running around Europe. My last semester of college, however, I realized that my friends meant more to me than any of this. After four years of chasing things, I realized that the people in my life brought me more joy than anything else. This gave me a sense of peace, a feeling that God's greatest gifts don't need to be hunted down and trapped.

But it didn't last. Just when I thought I had life figured out, the train went off the tracks again.

Two weeks before I was to graduate college, I was sitting in my friend Mark's room. It was late May, the end of springtime, warm but not too hot with a gentle breeze. I didn't feel like studying, even though finals were only days away. We were blasting music in Mark's room while I tried to convince him to break up with his girlfriend who, in my opinion, was only a few waves short of a shipwreck. He bobbed his head in time with the bass thundering out of his speakers, not really listening to me. Then his phone rang. Mark answered and got a puzzled look on his face.

"It's your dad," he said. "He called your room, and you weren't there so he traced you here."

"That's weird," I said and took the phone. "Hello?"

"Stephen, it's your dad." When my father talks to me on the phone, he usually calls me "Buddy." He doesn't use my full first name unless something's wrong.

"What's going on?"

"Son, I've got some bad news. Your friend Bill passed away yesterday. He got an asthma attack that wouldn't stop. They took him to the emergency room, and he went into heart failure. I'm afraid he's dead."

There's a reason cops and doctors learn fifty different ways to repeat those words. Your brain refuses to decipher them. I didn't understand what Dad said. It wasn't shock or denial; he spoke a foreign language. I asked Dad to repeat himself and he did. Then a heavy, numb feeling seeped into my body. I said good-bye to my dad, and, without saying a word to Mark, walked out of his room and back to my own. I shut the door and started screaming at God. I used so much profanity that I'm not even going to try and paraphrase what I said. I felt awful about it later, but at that moment, I didn't care. I was furious with God.

I was going to fly home for Bill's funeral, so I called my professors and told them I needed to turn in all my papers and take all my exams in the next forty-eight hours. I didn't even pose it as a request. I was a good student, and I could flunk my finals and still get C's in all my classes and graduate. It wouldn't even have mattered to me if I didn't graduate; I was going home. My professors were gracious, so I wrote a couple of crappy papers, took my finals without studying, and flew back to Lexington.

As soon as I got home, I threw on a suit and tie and went to the funeral home for visiting hours with my parents. I had performed this ritual at least a dozen times. My father was the seventh of eight children, and he and Mom didn't have me until they were in their late thirties. Coming in on the end of things, I grew up with death as a fixture in my extended family. A host of great aunts and uncles, distant cousins, and three of my grandparents had already departed the earth. I would get dressed up in uncomfortable clothes and watch old people proceed by another old person in a casket before gathering at someone's house to eat starchy food from casserole dishes.

So some things were familiar the night we went to see Bill—the dim lights, dark wooden pews, thick curtains, and beige carpet. The earnest staff and the organ music crackling out of speakers in the ceiling. Other than that, everything was different. More people milled around the casket. People I knew. Teachers, coaches, and friends walked haltingly up to the casket to say their good-byes. Some would cry; others would curse. Most just stared down at Bill, incredulous that one of our own lay in a place where we'd seen only our elders.

Bill's parents were nearby, hugging and shaking hands. Just like Bill, they were short and round. I had never seen them dressed up. I'd only caught glimpses of them in bathrobes and sweat suits as my friends and I ransacked their house. Their faces were red, and they looked stunned and exhausted. Bill's dad did his best to smile as he greeted everyone, but his mom didn't even try. She dabbed her eyes with a handkerchief, though no more tears came. I saw them as I walked through the door and tried to imagine what they were going through. I couldn't. I was in hell, but they were suffering even more.

My friends and I left our parents to pace around commiserating with each other as we huddled in a small room with a coffeemaker, hidden near the rear exit. We were weary from hearing the same condolences from everyone and wanted to be where no one could find us. We also wanted the secrecy so we could drink. Eddie had brought the Maker's Mark in a flask and started mixing bourbon and Cokes. I got lit, and my parents were none the wiser. A semester in London had turned me into a social drinker and smoker, but I became a regular user after Bill died.

None of us was ready to go see Bill. We tried talking about other things, tried joking, but it didn't work. The suffocating air of the funeral home forbade mirth. At last, Stan rallied us for the inevitable.

"We should go see him," he said.

Nobody said anything. Kevin sighed and stood up. Everyone else followed his lead, but Patrick had to pull me up. We threw our arms around each other and moved toward the coffin like a big amoeba. The crowd parted to let us pass. Those waiting in line moved aside as we gathered around the casket to see the body of our friend.

I didn't want to look and stayed in the back as long as I could. Kevin, John, and Eddie were in front with the girls between them. Becky and Kristin sobbed and buried their faces in the lapels on either side of them. Kevin wept; Eddie just gaped. I stayed behind frozen. I could only see Bill's hand through the crowd in front of me. His class ring, its ruby gem sparkling, adorned one finger. Kevin lifted the hand and started stroking it. Tears came to my eyes, but I still couldn't move.

Kevin wiped his face with a tissue and turned around.

"Come up here, Steve," he said. "It's okay."

I didn't want to move, but Kevin took me by the arm and put me next to Becky. She looked up, eyes black and wet with mascara, and pulled me toward her. Then I looked.

I had seen nothing like it before. All the old folks I'd seen laid to rest looked normal. The white skin, the makeup, the dressy clothes, and the jewelry made the elderly look peaceful in death. On Bill, it looked unnatural. He looked too neat. His suit was pressed and his hair was parted. Bill never looked like that in life. He had been boisterous, loud, sweaty, and dressed only in basketball clothes or jeans. My last look at him was a starched picture that I didn't want to see.

My chest thrust in and out, sucking in air to power my hundredth bawling session. Water and snot poured out my nose like a valve had broken in my head. I realized I hadn't brought a handkerchief and wiped my face with my coat sleeve. Stan pulled a clean hanky out of his coat and handed it over. My tears drenched it before Kevin finally pulled me away. I didn't want to go. I kept looking at Bill, searching for something to make me feel like he was still there. I gave up and stumbled to a chair, where I wiped my cheeks and refused all words of comfort.

The funeral the following morning was worse. The preacher giving the eulogy started talking about Bill being in heaven.

Bill believed in God, Jesus, the resurrection, and all the main points. He didn't go to church very often, but he'd told me that he prayed a lot. I knew, however, that Bill had never prayed "the sinner's prayer" that my Baptist teachers had told me was necessary to make it through the pearly gates.

I started bawling. I wasn't doing any of this masculine "moist eyes," either. Tears and snot were once again running down my face. Stan, without a word, passed me a handkerchief, which I promptly ruined. But I wasn't just crying out of sadness. My tears of mourning ran together with tears of anger. The mere thought that someone might think Bill was in hell enraged me. I hated the fact that I'd been taught something that would preclude my friend from heaven. In that moment, I decided that it wasn't true. Bill was in heaven because nothing made sense otherwise. I was furious that I'd been breastfed on a religion that would exclude someone from the presence of God based on one scripted prayer from a cheesy-looking tract.

Stan, Kevin, John, Patrick, Sulli, Eddie, and I were pallbearers. We piled into a limo after the funeral to go to the cemetery. The line of cars went on forever. We said nothing as Eddie passed a flask of bourbon around, and we took liberal slugs of the burning tonic. The driver noticed but didn't comment. The morning traffic came to a halt as a police escort guided the procession down Main Street, toward Lexington Cemetery. Henry Clay is buried there—it's a tourist attraction. As we approached, I saw the elder statesman's statue hovering above the trees. He stood on a pedestal with one foot in front of him, like he was about to leap off into the air.

When we arrived at the cemetery, we put our mourning on hold as the funeral director explained the logistics of carrying the casket from the hearse to the grave. The driver rolled the coffin out, and we took hold of the brass rails. The weight was staggering. I was terrified that I would trip or lose my grip and Bill's well-dressed body would fall out. I forgot the horror of carrying my friend to his final resting place. I could only think how mortified everyone would be if I fell on my butt.

We made it without dropping him and set the casket on a small metal scaffold over the grave. The minister gave a brief eulogy, but I didn't hear any of it. I stared at the box in front of me and couldn't believe that Bill was in there. I looked at the hole beneath it, covered with fake green turf, and couldn't believe that he would be down there in only a few hours. Everything was muted and slow, like I was underwater.

After the benediction, the guys and I filed out past the casket. We each placed a rose on top. Becky and Kristin stood nearby crying as they watched us file by. The crowd stood still. Someone played "Amazing Grace" on an electric organ. I heard isolated sobbing and people blowing their nose. A girl toward the rear was wailing at the top of her lungs. When the hymn ended, the crowd dispersed from the back.

We leaned against the limo and waited to leave. People lined up to console us like a receiving line at a wedding reception. Nothing anyone said helped. I got a lot of, "Let me know if there's anything I can do." I wanted to say, "I'll tell you what you can do. Bring Bill back like Jesus did Lazarus. Turn back time and change everything. If you can't do any of those things, leave me alone." But all I said was, "Please pray for Bill's family."

In the parking lot, Patrick gathered everyone together. He spread his arms and told everyone to huddle up. We gathered in a big group hug, embracing each other in a circle and spilling tears on the pavement of the funeral home parking lot.

"I don't want to lose anyone else," he said. "I don't mean just dying either. We have to be friends forever." We pulled each other close and tearfully agreed.

Bill's parents invited us to their house after the funeral. We went and ate starchy food from casserole dishes while making small talk with the adults. We went downstairs to Bill's room and cried some more. Eddie passed the flask around, and I was looped by two o'clock. It didn't cross my mind that I might be committing a sin. I didn't care.

All of a sudden, I was more cynical than ever. I despised any religion that peddled simple beliefs and pat answers. I was pissed off that nobody told me how complicated things really were. Most of all, I stopped believing that God would protect me from pain just because I was a good Christian. Life was a craps game, and God was just the stickman. Anyone who said different was either manipulative or stupid. I let all the joy God had given me through Bill and my other friends become a source of rage. I was in too much pain to be grateful for the gift God had given me in Bill. I told myself a bunch of lies about God being a callous, cruel deity instead of the benevolent king who'd placed Bill in my life.

After the funeral, I spent a couple more days in Lexington. I went out and got drunk with my friends each night. I'd wake up in the morning filled with sadness and anger, then count the hours until I went out with my friends that night. We talked about Bill, but we stuck to the funny stories, mostly. We kept our pain obscure and hazy with alcohol.

I went back to Wake Forest for "post-exams," a bacchanal

that was held every year at Myrtle Beach between the end of finals and graduation. I started drinking on the drive from Wake Forest and didn't stop for two more days. I did a lot of indiscriminate kissing with female "friends," yet another attempt to numb the fury of depression and confusion. Most of all, I didn't want to feel my anger toward God. It would be a long time before I understood that I had just as much to celebrate as I did to mourn.

• • •

A few years later, my phone rang on a Saturday afternoon. It was Eddie. I hadn't talked to him very much since Bill's death. Enjoying each other without Bill around had been difficult.

Ed told me that he was coming back to Lexington in a couple weeks for the spring horse racing season at Keeneland. He asked if I wanted to come. Until that moment, I didn't realize how badly I wanted to see Eddie and everybody else.

"I'm in," I said. "Who else is coming?"

"Everybody," he said.

"You've called everyone already? They've committed?"

"No," he said. "But they will if they know what's good for them."

Eddie was right. Everyone came home for a weekend. We even took a big group picture in Stan's back yard. I still have it. We spent all weekend telling each other how much we missed each other. We renewed our promise to be friends forever.

That's when I understood how much Bill had blessed us. His death had created a bond between those he left behind. That bond has never gone away. My friends and I have spent vacations and holidays together and stood in each other's weddings. We've been there for each other through marriage and money problems. Those guys are my brothers to this day. I haven't talked to any of them in weeks, but if I called any one of them right now, we'd be laughing in seconds. We wouldn't even bother to catch up for the first few minutes—we'd just talk smack and enjoy a rapport that's never gone away. I am thankful for that. I am grateful for the impact Bill had on my life and the way that he sanctified and solidified the friendships of those he left behind.

But I'd still rather have Bill back.

Yes, I grew because of Bill's death. Yes, Eddie, Kevin, Patrick, Stan, John, Becky, Kristin, and I are closer as a result. But those blessings are bittersweet. I would much rather have seen Bill at our twentieth high school reunion. I want to see his wife and children. I want to hear about his thrilling career in sports broadcasting. Why couldn't God have taught me some other way to value the people in my life? I'd rather have my friend back.

Of all the questions I want to ask when I get to heaven, number one on the list will be: "Why do you have to teach us things through suffering? Isn't there another way? Yeah, yeah, I understand why it works so well. I get that pain helps us learn things emotionally and experientially instead of just intellectually. But you are God. You could make it work any way you want! Why did you have to set things up like this?"

I'm sure God's answer will blow me away, and I'll feel all stupid and scared like Job in front of the whirlwind when God says, "Who is this that darkens my counsel with words without knowledge?" (Job 38:2 NIV). In the meantime, I'm still aggravated. And that's now, when the pain has mostly subsided.

When it happened, I was a cauldron of anger and despair. My cynicism about the church extended to God. I no longer trusted God and stopped talking to him.

Apparently, my bitter silence didn't have much of an effect, because God devised a plan to rescue my heart yet again. And he did it in a way that I never would have imagined. Though I no longer trusted God, God was about to show me that he still trusted me.

3

The Rise
and Fall of a
Youth Pastor

MEREDITH SAID IT WAS "FINE" IF I MOVED TO D.C. after college. Not awesome, great, super, cool, or even swell. Just "fine." After three and a half years of long-distance dating, I was hoping for a little more enthusiasm from my girlfriend at the prospect of us living in the same city. But I got about what I expected.

Meredith and I had met between my freshman and sophomore years of college, while I was on vacation with the guys at Myrtle Beach. We fell hard and fast for each other in the reckless way only a nineteen-year-old boy and eighteen-year-old girl can. We began a relationship even though she lived in Maryland and I lived in Kentucky and went to college in North Carolina. Like most long-distance relationships, it had been intense and romantic because there was no day-to-day intimacy. Our relationship was built on sophomoric love letters and whirlwind weekends. By my senior year, however, the passion had cooled, especially on her end. After Bill died, I felt lost and desperate and began clinging to my relationship with Meredith more than ever. I called too much and asked for reassurance all the time.

Maybe that's why she wasn't head over heels when I told her I wanted to move closer to her after college.

In order to make the move, I would need to spend the first few weeks living with my sister and her husband, Tom, in Alexandria, Virginia, a suburb of D.C. They were on staff at a Baptist church—busy people without the space and resources to stable a twenty-two-year-old man-child.

"You don't even have a job," Lisa told me over the phone as I pleaded with her to let me stay with them.

"I don't have a job *yet*," I corrected her. "I will soon. Then I'll find an apartment and move out."

"You and Meredith aren't planning on getting a place together, are you?"

"Are you on drugs?"

"Well, you never know ..."

"Yes, you do. When you're talking to me, you know better than that."

"Well, I guess it's fine if you stay with us for a little while. Just plan on being at church on Sunday mornings."

So the first thing I did after college was accept charity from my sister so I could live near my less-than-enthusiastic girlfriend. Not exactly a triumphant beginning to my post-college life, but it would suffice.

. . .

Mom and Dad gave me some money to get started, and I used that money to get my own place ASAP. I could only afford to rent somebody's basement, but it felt like a palace since it was the first place that I could ever call my own. I burned through the rest of Dad's money buying cheap furniture from Ikea and clothes for job interviews. After I'd been in my new place only two weeks, I realized that I'd moved out of my sister's place too soon because I was almost out of money. I needed a job quick, or I'd have to move back to Kentucky and live with my parents. The whole point of getting an education had been to move out of my parents' house so I could do whatever I wanted, whenever I wanted. Moving home would have represented a humiliating defeat. My parents would think I wasn't an adult yet. And I was convinced that if I got more than a hundred miles away from Meredith, our relationship was finished.

I looked at the classifieds every day and sent out dozens of résumés. Since I had pretty good grades in college, I got a few interviews, but most of them went like this one I had for a crisis counseling agency:

"So, you double-majored in psychology and religion?" queried the social worker who was interviewing me. "I see you graduated with honors. Looks like you worked hard in college."

"Yes, ma'am."

"Have you had any experience in crisis counseling before?"

"No, ma'am, but I want to be a psychologist someday, so I think it would be a great—"

"Would you be willing to intern for free?"

"I would love to if I could. I'm afraid I have to have an income."

"I see. Why don't you come back when you're serious enough about this type of work to intern for us."

Just when I was about to hit up the Olive Garden for a job waiting tables, I came across an opening for a youth pastor at a large Presbyterian church in D.C. A church advertising in the classifieds should have been my first warning sign. Why would any church serious about its youth ministry stick an ad in the newspaper? But I needed a job, and I was minimally qualified for this one. I'd double-majored in psychology and religion and my résumé boasted numerous experiences working with kids. If nothing else, I knew my way around a youth group after nearly living at church as an adolescent.

My reason for applying was not because I wanted a career in youth ministry. When I was in junior high, I'd thought about becoming a youth pastor, but the Jeff era squelched that dream. Furthermore, I still wasn't on speaking terms with God because of Bill's death. But I needed a job.

I sent in a résumé and followed up with a phone call, doubtful that anything would come of it. No way God was going to trust me with this kind of gig. I'd shot a bunch of four-letter words at the guy only a few weeks earlier. I was surprised a lightning bolt hadn't found its way to the ground via my spinal cord yet. So when the church called me to set up an interview, I was shocked. Why would God want me—in my discombobulated spiritual condition—shepherding a bunch of kids? How was I supposed to provide spiritual guidance to any kid, much less a whole throng of them?

But I still needed a job.

My brother-in-law Tom, a veteran youth minister, and my sister Lisa, a minister of education and a former youth pastor herself, helped me prepare for the interview. They told me what questions to ask and the best answers to give. Thanks to them, I was equipped to come off like a pro as long as nobody looked too closely.

The morning of the interview, I donned my best suit and

blared U2 from the speakers of the used Oldsmobile that my parents bought me for graduation. I almost pulled out into traffic, then suddenly thought about where I was going. I turned off the radio and dropped my forehead onto the steering wheel. *If you want me to do this,* I prayed, talking to God for the first time in three months, *okay, I guess. I have no idea what you're up to, but maybe it's time for me to try trusting you again. Just don't give me this job if it's not in your will. I'm desperate for a job, but I can't do this without your help. But if I do get it … well, I just hope you know what you're doing.*

I got the job, but I still wasn't convinced that God knew what he was doing.

· · ·

During my first week as a youth pastor, the secretary handed me a letter. She said it was from a woman named Jane who had my job about ten years ago. I opened it and started reading. Like over half of the letters I received every day, it presented a ministry opportunity for the youth group. Jane was an associate pastor for a church in Baltimore, and she suggested we get our youth groups together and visit a monastery that had a potato farm. She said we could spend the night there and the kids could spend the day gleaning potatoes.

I'm going to have enough trouble getting kids to come to church as it is, I thought. *I don't think spending a Saturday digging potatoes out of the ground is going to set any new attendance records.* Not the most service-minded attitude, I admit, but I was young and still figuring things out. The letter read like an open-ended offer and didn't ask for a reply, so I stuck it in a file and forgot about it.

The first time I met with my new adolescent flock, I introduced myself and told them we were going to open in prayer. They looked at me like I said we were going to eat live pigeons.

"Why are we praying?" asked a thin girl with glasses.

"You guys don't usually do this?"

"No. Why would we?"

I didn't even have a good answer for her. I just took it for granted that you opened and closed in prayer whenever engaging in organized religion. But I was fast enough on my feet. "It's good to invite God into our presence. It lets him know that we want him to guide us and bless what we do." That drew some strange looks, but nobody protested.

The youth in my charge were accustomed to playing games, talking about current events, and griping about school. That's good stuff, but I wasn't about to be a youth minister that didn't pray and talk about Jesus. I realized that I was going to have to begin with the basics. At Bible study that week, I started with Jesus.

"Who knows why Jesus died on the cross?"

Blank stares.

"Does anyone want to guess?"

The thin girl with glasses raised her hand. "To show us that it's good to die for important causes?" Her voice went up at the end of the sentence, making it a question.

Uh-oh, I thought. *This is gonna be a lot of work.*

It was, but I was equal to the task. I knew what to teach these kids. Years of fundamentalist upbringing had emblazoned the Bible and Christian theology on my brain. My bachelor's in religion refined that knowledge and gave it academic heft.

Also, I needed the task. When I realized that these kids hadn't heard the full gospel, I pulled my head out of my own self-pitying butt long enough to realize that there was more at stake than my grievances and personal suffering. I was desperate for help and started looking to God again to find it.

One Wednesday afternoon, I was preparing for Bible study that evening. I was flipping through John because I'd always heard that was a good book for introducing people to the gospel. I started reading at the beginning, thinking about which passages I would use in explaining the plan of salvation. I was thinking about what I was going to say to the kids, but by the time I got to John 3:6–8, I was reading for me instead of them.

> Flesh gives birth to flesh, but the Spirit gives birth to spirit. You should not be surprised at my saying, "You must be born again." The wind blows wherever it pleases. You hear its sound, but you cannot tell where it comes from or where it is going. So it is with everyone born of the Spirit.

Goose pimples spread across my forearms. A thought intruded my consciousness, "You need to be born again."

I'd been brought up to believe that being "born again" was a one-time deal. You got saved and that was it. All you had to do was kick back, behave yourself, and wait for heaven. Now I realized that Jesus was talking about something else. Being born again means being born of the Holy Spirit. It means living the life of the Spirit. And the life of the Spirit is like the wind, wild and unpredictable. I had stopped living that life. When Bill died, I didn't want to ride the wind anymore. It was too scary. I wouldn't let the Spirit toss me around if it meant I might get hurt. I expected God to protect me, not send me on Mr. Toad's Wild Ride of the Spirit. So I abandoned the life of the Spirit and gave in to depression. But now I wanted to ride again. I wanted to be born again, again.

I got on my knees and told God that I wanted to be born of the Spirit once more. I wanted the Holy Spirit back. I told God that I still didn't really trust him completely, but it felt like that was actually part of the deal. I didn't know where God was going to take me, and I knew it might involve pain. But I understood that the life of the Spirit worked that way.

"I don't really trust you, God," I said. "But I guess I'm trusting you even in my lack of trust, if that makes any sense. I want to ride the wind again. I want you to be in charge of my life again."

I got off my knees and took a deep breath. I felt calmness I hadn't known in months. I smiled and got back to preparing for Bible study.

I began praying 'round the clock, and my hunger for God returned. As I built a foundation of faith for my kids, I was rebuilding mine. I started to recover the simple truths of my faith: loving and serving others, forgiveness, salvation, the sustaining presence of the Holy Spirit, and guidance through the Bible. I conducted an archeological dig of my own faith. I broke through layers of cynicism and pain left by Bill's death, my conflicts with Brother Jeff, and the overintellectualizing of my faith in college. I excavated the pure, elemental aspects of my faith that had set me on fire as a kid. I was still angry with God over Bill's death, but that now stood next to a gospel that I could not deny no matter how mad I was. That's what I learned when God shoved me into being a youth pastor. He showed me that I could depend on him even though we hadn't resolved all our issues.

. . .

I was overjoyed at my renewed relationship with God. I felt like a new man, lifted up by the wind of the Spirit. My months-long depression dissipated, and I became a much nicer guy to be around. I was eager to share this joy with someone other than the teenagers in my youth group. Who better than my girlfriend?

Meredith came back from college over Thanksgiving, and we had plans to spend Saturday together. She arrived three hours late. I had fallen asleep on the couch. I'd left the door unlocked and she let herself in. I woke up and saw her sitting on the edge of the couch.

"How long have you been sitting there?" I asked.

"I don't know," she said. "A few minutes, maybe."

"What took you so long? Our whole day is—"

"I want to break up," she said.

I rubbed the sleep from my eyes and said, "What?"

"We're breaking up," she said. "I didn't want to do it over the phone."

My anger operates in reverse compared to most people. I don't gradually get upset and then lose my temper. I lose my temper first, even though I calm down pretty fast after that. Regardless, I blew up in Meredith's face. I didn't call her names or throw things; I just yelled a lot.

"What the—I saw you just a month ago, and everything was fine!"

"I'm not happy," she said.

"Don't you think that would be something to bring up before you decided to dump me? You don't want to work things out? You just want to bolt?"

"Yes. My decision is final."

The rest of the conversation went on just like that. I gave long, angry diatribes and Meredith responded in three-word sentences, all of which spelled doom for our three-and-a-half-year relationship. When I was convinced that there was no changing her mind, I told her to leave. No good-bye, no call me later; I just showed her the door. Then, for the first time since I'd become a youth pastor, I drove to the store and bought a pack of cigarettes. I stayed up until four o'clock in the morning, smoking, praying, and talking to friends on the phone.

Though Meredith's decision blindsided me at the time, I should have seen it coming. I saw signs that she was unhappy, and I'd been in denial. We started dating when she was eighteen and I was nineteen. We were now twenty-one and twenty-two. People change a lot in those three years, shuffling off adolescence to form an adult identity. We had grown apart, but I had clung to the relationship harder than ever. I was relying on her to meet too many of my needs. I'd left behind a sturdy support system in college. I'd been in a fraternity and active in InterVarsity Christian Fellowship. I had unlimited access to friends, fun, and the sort of deep, abstract talk you get only in college. Now I lived alone in a basement apartment, and my primary social outlet was a bunch of teenagers. My girlfriend was in her senior year of college, hours away with a different life. It strained her to be my only significant adult relationship. I pestered her with phone calls and pleas for reassurance about the stability of our relationship. Imagining the fun she was having on weekends while I was home alone staring at the wall, I became suspicious about the other guys in her life. The strain was too much for her, so she mustered the courage to end our relationship. Though I thought she was crazy at the time, it was the right thing to do.

I only had a couple of friends in D.C. I wasn't involved in anything outside of my job. After Meredith broke up with me, I fled back to North Carolina to be close to friends for a few days. When I got back to D.C. on a Saturday, I stopped by the church to check messages before heading home. I opened the door of my office and gasped.

Everything was covered in newspaper. Not just the walls and the furniture, but everything on my desk. My stapler and every pen were wrapped tightly in newsprint. Someone had taken each book off my shelf, wrapped it in newspaper, and put it back in place. After the shock wore off, a grin spread across my face. Then I started laughing, as my post-break-up stupor started to lift. The kids in my youth group had done this. They weren't going to let me have a week off without making me pay for it.

"Thanks, God," I said. "You've given me so much more here than I realize. You knew exactly what I needed. Thank you for this job and these amazing kids."

I started unwrapping my office. By the time I finished, my hands were black.

The next few weeks with the kids were bliss. My love for them grew, their trust in me increased, and more kids started coming to Christ. Sometimes I would offer specific opportunities for them to give their lives to Christ, but most of the time, God just surprised me.

One day, a big, burly guy named Mike started showing up to youth group. He didn't talk much until he found out that I'd been on the wrestling team in high school. He was a wrestler too, and it created an immediate bond. Wrestling is a bit of a novelty sport, so it's like wrestlers are in a secret fraternity. Mike started hanging around after Bible study to talk about his matches. We never talked about God. Then, one day he asked if he could chat with me in my office. Such a request wasn't unusual, even from the kids I didn't know well. It was often the result of a romantic crisis. Someone got their heart broken and came to me for help picking up the pieces. But that's not what Mike wanted.

"I've been thinking that I want to accept Jesus as my Savior. Can you help me with that?"

I smiled.

"Yeah, man," I said. "I can help you with that."

We prayed together as Mike asked Jesus to forgive his sins and come into his heart. We talked for a while after, going over some ways to get started on the most amazing journey of his life. Then we talked about wrestling. When he left, I praised God. I even stuck my hands in the air, which is not something I do.

I rediscovered the foundational truth that I taught my kids: God came to earth as a man; preached justice, peace, and wisdom; died on a cross for our sins; and rose from the dead—all so we could have forgiveness and a relationship with the creator of the universe, ours for the asking. It's an impossible, glorious, beautiful, and dangerous truth. Maybe the whole youth group hadn't experienced revival, but more and more kids over the next few months discovered Jesus and began a relationship with him. Their joy and wonder helped me recover some of mine.

. . .

Though I was relishing my revived relationship with God and rejoicing in the increasing faith of the youth group, I still felt a little lost. Some of the popular kids didn't like me because I was "too Christian" (What did they expect to find at a Presbyterian church? A goat worshiper?). Several times I caved in to their desires to hold more fluff-filled activities. I occasionally turned a blind eye to inappropriate behavior because I didn't want to be a disciplinarian; I wanted to be the cool youth pastor. And I wasn't great at outreach either. I was good at making friends with kids once they showed up at church, but I didn't want to seem pushy with kids who didn't already attend. In other words, I was preoccupied with everyone liking me. Maybe it was because I didn't have many friends in the area and my girlfriend had just skated on me. All of my positive reinforcement came from the kids, and I didn't want to lose that.

Frank and the rest of the staff weren't helping this situation very much. I was running the youth program without any guidance, unsure if I was doing things right.

"You're a bright spot here at church," Frank, the senior pastor, said when I got back from our fall high school retreat. I grinned and thanked him, but didn't know what else to say. Frank showered me with weekly doses of sunshine, which were fun to soak up, but what I needed was direction. I was twisting in the wind most of the time, with little guidance from the rest of the staff.

"So, what do you want me to do with the youth budget surplus?" I would ask Frank. "Should I spend it, or does it go back into the general budget?"

"Don't worry about it," he said, as always. "We'll figure something out. You're doing fine."

Six months later, I hadn't figured anything out, and I was not doing fine. I had no idea what I was doing. I knew the Bible and I could handle teenagers pretty well, but I had zero understanding of what it meant to be on a church staff. I didn't understand the chain of command, church politics, or how I was supposed to set and meet goals. I had little notion of what was expected of me.

"Frank, can I set up a time for an evaluation?" I asked, because I'd been on the job for six months with no substantial feedback. "I feel like I'm over my head here, and I need some guidance. Can you tell me what I need to do differently to make this work?"

Frank winked. "See, that's what I like about you. You take initiative."

He set the meeting up for a week later. We talked about theology for an hour and never got around to my job performance. The most useful thing I figured out was how to decode Frank-speak. When he made a "suggestion," it was merely an idea. When he made a "recommendation," it was a direct order. Good to know.

I had to set a vision and course for the youth group on my own. During my job interview, Frank had told me that one of his top priorities was starting a youth choir. At our next staff meeting, I told everyone that I was making a youth choir my number-one priority. Frank's eyes got wide and his mouth popped open, like a four-year-old catching Santa coming down the chimney.

"That's wonderful!" he said. "I know just the person you should contact about directing the choir," he said. "Betty Wilkes is the high school chorus teacher who used to be an active member at the church. She would be a great person to talk to." Finally! A concrete suggestion! I was so excited I called Mrs. Wilkes as soon as I left the meeting.

We talked for over an hour. We both got more excited as we talked. By the end of the call, I had an awesome plan for starting a youth choir. We were going to practice at the high school after classes. It would be an incredible outreach opportunity. I was certain it would increase our numbers by twenty percent and more kids would come to Christ. As a bonus, Mrs. Wilkes was an award-winning chorus teacher. We were going to sound great.

The next week, I skipped into staff meeting, ready to present my plan. I expected Frank to be so happy that he'd pop a blood vessel. I fidgeted in my chair as I waited for my turn to talk. When my turn came, I told the whole staff about how we were going to start a youth choir that would revitalize our entire youth ministry. I did my best to anticipate any questions and answer them in advance. I concluded by saying, "Mrs. Wilkes said she's ready to start in two months, right after Christmas." That should have been enough to make Frank so excited that he'd vomit a little bit in his mouth. I sat in silence, waiting for accolades.

Nobody said anything. The associate pastor shifted in his chair. The music minister looked at me with a pitying smile. Frank finally broke the silence.

"I don't think that's going to work," he said.

I said nothing, but the expression on my face told Frank all he needed to know.

"I'm sure you're disappointed," he said. "It sounds like you were excited. But you don't want to work with Mrs. Wilkes. She's too strong for you."

"But you told me to ask her to do it!" I said, too shocked and angry to play at being deferential.

"I told you to talk to her," he said. "I didn't say I wanted her to lead the choir."

The silence in the room was loud. Everyone just stared at me. Some people gave me sympathetic looks. Others seemed to watch me in anticipation, wondering if they'd get a chance to see me cry. I just said nothing because there was nothing to say. I knew, because I'd been here before. It was Jeff the Carrot all over again. Logic had gone out the window. Frank didn't want Mrs. Wilkes to lead the choir? Didn't he regard this piece of information as something to share with me before he sent me to talk to her about starting a cotton-pickin' youth choir?

Frank consoled me a little more in front of everyone and then adjourned the meeting. What Frank didn't know is that he'd just helped me make some decisions about the Christmas holidays. I was getting paid ten thousand dollars a year for twenty hours a week, but I was really working thirty or forty. If you threw in retreats and lock-ins, it was closer to fifty or sixty. I deserved a break. I didn't take Frank's "suggestion" to help with the Advent services and went back to Kentucky for Christmas. I also decided to cancel the New Year's Eve lock-in when I found out that most of the youth group would be attending a party that one of the popular kids was throwing. I accepted an invitation from my college buddy Jimmy to go to New York City and watch the ball drop in Times Square. I had the time of my life, which convinced me that canceling the lock-in had been a good move.

When I got back from the holidays, there was plenty to keep me busy: two ski trips, a retreat, and a mission trip to Mexico in the spring. Kids were coming to Jesus like the rapture was going to happen any minute. I started to forget about Meredith. Frank still drove me a little crazy, but my time with the kids made up for that. I had planned on only taking one or two years off after college before heading to grad school, but I started to imagine myself remaining at the church for five years or more. I was starting to feel more comfortable in my role. I didn't feel as intimidated by the popular kids. It felt like I was learning ways to navigate around Frank. I was becoming more assertive and developing a vision for the youth group. I was excited about becoming better at my job. It felt like I'd found my place, and I wanted to stay for a while.

◦ ◦ ◦

On a Monday, Frank told me to schedule a meeting with him for Friday afternoon. He told me that he wanted to talk about ways we could improve the church's youth center. He asked me to research how other churches had turned their facilities into community centers and places where people could stay during mission trips and the like. I ran all over Washington, D.C., interviewing church staff and touring buildings. I showed up for our meeting with a thick manila folder filled with notes, brochures, and an outline for how we could enhance our youth center. Frank told me to set the folder aside.

"Steve, we won't be renewing your contract for next year."

Does that mean what I think it means, I thought. *Surely it doesn't.*

"You mean you're firing me?" I said.

"We won't be renewing your contract next year."

Apparently, Frank and Meredith had taken the same class on how to ax somebody. Just repeat the same thing over and over again until the person spontaneously combusts.

"Let me get this straight—I won't be working here next year."

"That's right."

The anger bomb went off inside me, but I had to keep my cool.

"I'm outraged," I said without raising my voice. "And I want an explanation."

Frank proceeded to tell me, with more conviction than I'd seen in most of his sermons, the reasons I wasn't a good youth pastor.

First, he said that I was not a charismatic leader. He said that I wasn't good at planning and executing programs. He said that I was a "mystic," like a Jedi Knight, I guess, without the cool powers. Other than that, he only gave three specific reasons for canning me: (1) I didn't get a youth choir going, which was one of my main goals, (2) I hadn't returned a letter from a former youth pastor inviting us to glean potatoes at a monastery, and (3) I hadn't held the annual youth lock-in on New Year's Eve.

The youth choir thing almost made my head explode. I had arranged everything for an amazing youth choir, and Frank had killed it. And that stupid letter hadn't asked for a reply, and it was a lame idea, anyway. And who the heck gets fired for not answering one letter? Of course, I didn't find out until that moment that the author was a longtime friend of Frank's. That would have been good to know. It would have also helped to know that she was a tattletale.

The absence of a New Year's Eve lock-in was my fault, however. This brings me to the reason that I deserved to be fired—I let fear get in the way of my job. I canceled the New Year's Eve lock-in because one of the popular kids in the youth group was having a party at her house. That was nothing more than stupid insensitivity on my part. It didn't occur to me that some of the less popular kids wouldn't get invited. They needed a place to go, and I had denied them of that. Frank had me nailed on that one.

Oh, and Frank telling me I'm a "mystic" instead of a charismatic leader and a good administrator? Fear caused that too. At the time, I blamed it on Frank not spending enough time with me, but the blame is mine. I never let Frank, or anyone else, see what I could really do because I was afraid of taking risks. I have leadership gifts that Frank didn't see because I was afraid to put myself out front. He sensed that he wasn't getting the real Steve, so he had to fire the fake one. It was a good call.

Though I'd learned to depend on God again, I still didn't trust him completely. I played things safe. Just as I insisted on nothing but peace and security at my church when I was a kid, I tried to have the same thing when I worked at a church. I didn't want to do anything that kids didn't like. I was too sensitive to the whims of the popular kids who held the most influence. I would go to football games at the high school, but I was afraid to strike up conversation with the kids unless they approached me. I didn't want to risk looking foolish, even though that's a basic requirement for youth ministry. In church staff meetings, I followed everyone else's lead instead of offering my own ideas. I couldn't handle it when my suggestions were shot down. I retreated into the background, waiting for someone else to tell me what to do. When Frank shot down my youth choir plan, I didn't even push back. I didn't ask to talk to him in private. I just wilted like a wet noodle. No wonder the guy couldn't see what I was producing. I took no initiative and chose the path of least resistance most of the time. As a result, the youth program didn't grow. The kids who were already there got to know Jesus a lot better, but we didn't reach many new ones.

It's no wonder Frank thought I was a mystic. I kept my mouth shut all the time. It wasn't because I was praying or meditating—I was scared. Anyone who knows me even a little wouldn't call me a mystic. I'm impulsive, impatient, opinionated, and loud. If the real Steve had shown up at that church, nobody would have mistaken him for a monk. And the real Steve would have been a much better youth pastor. So—the youth choir and that silly letter aside—I deserved to get fired. In fact, it wasn't even me that got fired. The milquetoast, frightened, self-pitying version of me got the boot. And it taught me that it's much better to be yourself and take risks than to hide behind your fears and hope nobody sees you.

I am thankful that God made me a youth pastor. I'm thankful that Frank fired me. Heck, I'm even thankful for Frank. It's so unfair what my cynical filter does to people who hurt me—it turns them into monsters, into enemies. Just as Brother Jeff cared for me, so did Frank. Even though I was angry with him for years, he gave me gifts. I gained wisdom under his training. He sharpened me. Most of us think of iron sharpening iron (Proverbs 27:17) as polite conversation or spirited debate at most. What we don't realize is that we teach one another wisdom even when we hurt each other. We learn how to love in the midst of brokenness and imperfection. Those who hurt us sometimes teach us far more than those who love us. Sometimes they're even the same person. Those we care about have the greatest capacity to hurt us. Love creates the possibility of pain like nothing else.

It's just like our relationship with God.

Ever since I walked down the aisle of a Baptist church when I was seven years old, I have been in love with Jesus. That's why he makes me crazy. He does things I don't understand. He puts me in situations that terrify me. I don't understand it, and it irritates the crap out of me, but I still love him. I also know that he loves me far more than I love him, which is why I break his heart so often. But he still loves me.

Frank, just like Jeff, wrote me a letter after I was gone. He told me that I had a profound impact on the kids. He said that my commitment to Christ was evident, and I handled getting fired with grace (great acting job, that). He said that he would miss me. And he said something else I'll never forget because it infuriated me at the time: "I think God has got great plans for you. You have a passionate faith and many gifts."

Frank knew that he wasn't getting the real Steve. Maybe God wanted more than the scared, cynical shadow of what he created me to be. Maybe that's why his next assault of joy was particularly brutal. And beautiful.

4

A Little
Death and
Resurrection

RIGHT AFTER I LOST MY JOB, I MOVED TO CHARLOTTE, North Carolina, because my best friend from college, Mark, needed a roommate. I went without a job. I had the option to move back in with Mom and Dad, but I wasn't ready to submit to what had become a cliché for my generation.

Within a month of arriving in Charlotte, I got a job as an Admissions Counselor at Belmont Abbey College. This kind of work was exactly what I needed—a low-stress job that gave me the opportunity to travel and meet other people my age. On my extended recruiting trips, I ran around New York, Philadelphia, and Boston visiting high schools and going to college fairs. My job was to get the surly youth of the Northeast to trade their big cities and bagels for presweetened tea (and people) in North Carolina. When I wasn't on the road, Mark and I had a blast being bachelors in Charlotte. I got involved in a Bible study and started to feel okay about just being a church member again. The year I spent in Charlotte was the only time that felt like I was really in my twenties. I had no real responsibility, no girl-friend, just enough money, and plenty of time for fun. I felt like an adult but I didn't feel old.

I wasn't going to make a career out of college admissions, however. Ever since my sophomore year of college, I had wanted to become a psychologist. I even knew where I wanted to go to graduate school: Fuller Theological Seminary.

Fuller looked like heaven on paper. They had a six-year program that would earn me a PhD in Clinical Psychology and an MA in Theology. I'd be able to bring my two favorite disciplines together as a Christian counselor. Even better, Fuller was somewhere I'd dreamed of living my entire life: Southern California. I hated cold weather, and so many things I loved—from music to movies to edgy Christian scholars—came from SoCal. I spent days working on my application, sent it in, and waited what felt like an eternity for Fuller's decision.

On a Monday night in April, the phone rang while I was in the bathroom. Mark pounded on the door and said that the phone was for me.

"Are you out of your friggin' mind?" I shouted through the door. "Take a message! I'm kinda busy in here."

"You want to take this call, dude," said Mark.

I elongated my body just enough to open the door and stick a hand through. Mark handed me the phone and I slammed the door in his face.

"Hello?" I demanded.

"Stephen?" said a mature female voice that I didn't recognize.

"Yes, ma'am?"

"Did I catch you at a bad time?"

"Um, no ma'am. May I ask who's calling?"

"This is Bert Jacklitch, Director of Operations at Fuller Theological Seminary's School of Psychology."

"Hi," I said, because I didn't know what else to say while sitting on the toilet on the verge of a nervous breakdown.

"We'd like to offer you a place in our Clinical Psychology PhD program this fall."

"Yes!" I shouted and launched off the toilet into the air. Bert started laughing on the other end.

"I take it this is good news," she said.

I thanked her about a hundred times. All my dreams were about to come true. I was going to move to Los Angeles and let Fuller turn me into a well-heeled guru who dispenses edgy Christian wisdom from a comfortable chair. Of course, I would find a wife along the way—a gentle woman with grace and wisdom and looks to die for. God had finally paved an easy path before me, and I was eager to begin the blissful journey.

As if I hadn't been living my life long enough to know better.

. . .

On my first day of orientation at Fuller Theological Seminary's Graduate School of Psychology, I was standing in line for a buffet the school had spread for the newbies. I turned and saw a cute woman behind me. She smiled, and I said hi and introduced myself. Two minutes later, we were having a great conversation—we were covering psychology and faith and turning up all kinds of similar interests.

After we both got our food, she said, "Do you mind if I sit with you for lunch? I haven't really met anyone else yet."

"That sounds great," I said. Things were finally breaking my way. The three-year romantic drought that had come after

Meredith was about to end. It would soon be raining intelligent, soulful, blonde women just like this one.

We sat at a large round table with a gaggle of other neophytes. It was all smiles and introductions. Someone asked my new lady friend if she grew up in Southern California.

"No," she said. "My husband and I ..."

I didn't hear the rest of the sentence. The last time I was in school, it had been unnecessary to check for a wedding ring before beginning courtship maneuvers. I had just learned the hard way to add this to my repertoire.

I turned my attention to the faculty member sitting at our table. He seemed more intent on his food than anything else, but I decided to break the ice anyway.

"So what can a first-year student look forward to in the PhD program?"

"Why did you apply to the program?" he asked.

"I'm interested in counseling. I've wanted to become a psychologist for a while. I really like the idea of helping people through therapy."

"That's too bad," he said. "The program is very research oriented."

"I understand," I said. "I'm excited about doing research, but won't that inform my work as a clinician?"

"The program is very research oriented," he said and returned his attention to his food.

Things are getting off to a bad start, that's all, I told myself. *Fuller is going to be great. I just need to give it time.*

That's what I told myself.

I thought going to graduate school was going to turn my life around in every respect. First, I'd imagined that it would be a lot easier to find a girlfriend at a Christian graduate school. I thought there would be scores of smart, cute, Christian girls who must not be too legalistic if they're studying psychology. Such women were indeed found aplenty at Fuller. They just all happened to be married.

The cost and the classes didn't help. Nowadays, Fuller is a gentle, postmodern feel-good kind of place. The faculty and staff want the students to learn, but they also want them to feel valued and cared for. The professors are sensitive and they try not to overburden students with unreasonable assignments. When I matriculated, however, the last of the old guard was still hanging around. If you asked a stupid question in class, they told you so. They assigned a couple hundred pages of reading a night and didn't care that you had two part-time jobs. It was an old-school, stoic, academic environment.

Cynics are not fans of authority, so you can imagine how I reacted to the never-ending hurdles of the program. I griped to anyone who would listen about doing busy work, becoming somebody's research slave, and sitting through lectures that didn't pretend to have structure or a main point. Most of all, however, I howled about paying money for this drudgery. The balance of my student loans continued to grow until it looked like the military budget of some small, hostile country. For the first time, I had to foot the bill for my own education. Mom and Dad had ponied up a lot of money to get me through Wake Forest, but Fuller cost more and the program was longer. They helped out as much as they could, but I was mostly on my own. The idea that I was *paying* for what I regarded as academic hazing pushed every anti-authority button in my addled brain. As a large, faceless academic institution with ties to the church,

Fuller became the perfect target for years of pent-up aggravation and resentment. Fuller became Frank and Jeff. And since I had no chance at romance without breaking the tenth commandment, I also projected Meredith and any other woman who'd jilted me onto Fuller's female population.

I behaved like I was the victim and Fuller was the perpetrator. Fuller embodied something I'd been wrestling with for almost twenty years: institutional Christianity. Hardly a day went by when I wasn't pissed off at Fuller for something. Every bitter feeling I'd ever had about God and religion swelled and burst from my skin. I started calling myself an existentialist and balked at the word "evangelical," sometimes even the word "Christian." The baby had finally gone out with the bathwater.

The worst part about slogging my way through the barren landscape of graduate school was doing it alone. After two months at Fuller I'd made some acquaintances but no real friends. Everyone else seemed wide-eyed and energetic, as if they felt lucky to be there. They said things like "praise the Lord" a lot and smiled too much for my taste. I didn't have much patience for such folks, thinking them naive to be so happy in such an oppessive place. I spent my early weeks at Fuller calling friends back East, asking when they could come out and visit.

As a loner and a malcontent, I sat in the back row during class. After a few weeks, I noticed that another guy my age was usually back there with me. One day, we ended up sitting next to each other. About fifteen minutes into the lecture, a piece of paper edged onto my desk.

I could learn more watching Sesame Street, the note read.

I grinned and picked up the paper.

I would if I could afford a television set, I scribbled and handed the note back to him.

He smiled and we both went back to pretending to pay attention to our professor.

After class, I introduced myself.

"I'm Steve," I said.

"I'm Ryan. You feel like going over to McCormick and Schmick's for happy hour? They have beers for a buck and cheap appetizers."

He had me at "beers for a buck."

Ryan and I spent the next two hours surrounded by mahogany and green leather in the bar at McCormick and Schmick's. The room was warm and inviting, like something from a hunting lodge or a men's club. There was even a picture of George Patton in the restroom. Against all hope, the happy hour menu was within my budget. Ryan and I washed down massive, savory cheeseburgers with cold pints of Henry Weinhard's, wallowing in luxurious poverty.

Within minutes, Ryan and I discovered that we had a lot in common: the same taste in music and movies, a distaste for legalism, almost identical senses of humor, and similar sentiments about Fuller.

"So, how do you like it here?" I asked.

"It's okay," he said. " People are a little too conservative for me. Christians in Oregon are a bit more relaxed. I'm also one of like three Catholics in the whole school."

"The thing that kills me is how much money we have to pay. I wonder if it's going to be worth it."

"I have a twenty-hour job on top of school and I have to

share an apartment with three friends from Oregon who want to become actors," Ryan said.

"I know what you mean," I said. "I was hoping to have more fun."

"Me too. Folks down here need to figure out that there more ways to have fun than singing praise songs and eating ice cream."

"Maybe we could do something about that," I said.

Ryan smiled and looked at me for a few seconds.

"Maybe we should," he said.

"Forties and Follies." That's what we called it. Ryan and I decided that Fuller Follies, the seminary's annual student-produced variety show, would be more fun if we both drank a forty-ounce bottle of malt liquor before we went. Of course, we would have preferred something higher quality, like a nice microbrew, but we couldn't afford it. So we drank our giant $2.50 bottles of booze and walked to campus. We weren't wasted, but we weren't sober either. As we entered Travis Auditorium, two guys were playing acoustic guitars and singing a funny song. With the parts of my brain that inhibit stupid behavior drowning in malt liquor, I shouted the first thing that came to mind.

"Freebird!"

That got a laugh from the crowd, so I yelled it again. This time I heard only a couple of awkward chuckles. I was just sober enough to take this as a sign to keep my mouth shut for the rest of the show.

When Fuller Follies was over, I hung around and mingled in the crowd. I still had a buzz so I was louder than usual. I recognized a woman in the crowd that I had a crush on. I rushed over and gave her a hug. We were friends who'd hugged before, so I wasn't overstepping. But when she pulled back from the embrace, she looked at me with a cocked eyebrow and said, "You smell like you've been drinking."

Uh-oh. I'd forgotten that malt liquor doesn't exactly have a subtle aroma. Embarrassed, I mumbled something about having a beer with dinner and slunk away. As I turned around, I bumped into someone and came face to face with *him*. It was my client. Not just any client, but my first therapy client ever. First-year students saw one client for ten weeks so they could practice being a shrink. Now I was nose to nose with mine, with breath that had the pungency of my old fraternity house after a party. I tried to act like I didn't recognize him, but he put a hand on my shoulder.

"Hi!" he said. "How's it going?"

Not only did I reek of malt liquor, but our professors had told us that we weren't allowed to talk to our clients outside of therapy.

"Hey!" I said and kept moving.

"See you next week, I guess," he said.

"You bet," I said and fled the scene.

It was May and I'd been on a downward spiral since returning to school from Christmas break. I stopped being a "social smoker" and took up a full-time habit. I didn't drink alone and I only "partied" once or twice a week, but when I did imbibe, beer stocks soared on Wall Street. On top of that, I was openly contentious and controversial, even with people I'd just met. Instead of debating people who disagreed with me, I mocked them. I enjoyed shocking people and went out of my way to be a nonconformist. I also started having, in the lingo of my peers, "random hookups." These were PG-13 one-night stands. I'd make out with a woman who was my friend (at most), with no intention of pursuing a committed relationship. Though my grades were good and I kept up appearances in class, my personal life was out of control. I was angry, apathetic, and anxious, though I tried hard to hide that last one.

All this hedonistic rage disguised an intense dread. I started feeling afraid for reasons I didn't understand. This happened mostly when I was home alone. My apartment was small and Spartan and in a bad part of town. We didn't have much furniture and my roommate once said that spending a few days at our place could give someone an idea of what prison is like. My private pain reared its head in this solitary place. When I didn't have anything to do (or didn't feel like doing homework), I called friends to see if they wanted to hang out or just talk. If I couldn't locate anyone, I started to fidget. I'd head out to the balcony and have a cigarette to pass the time. The nicotine mingled with my ennui, making my heart beat faster. Then I would start sweating. These weren't full-blown panic attacks, just waves of anxiety. I felt alone and helpless. I had irrational fears about money, marriage, and career, what psychologists call "predicting the future." I could usually suppress my anxiety when I was around other people, but it gradually became worse and worse when I was alone. My schoolwork started to suffer and I stopped exercising. My normally healthy appetite for food was replaced by a craving for cigarettes, so I lost weight even though I wasn't exercising. It felt like I was living in this small, hot box from which nothing could release me. Cigarettes, and sometimes alcohol, were all that gave me peace. I prayed incessantly, but God didn't seem to be listening. I wondered if Jesus was content that I remain in pain and withheld all divine intervention on purpose.

Prayers, church services, the Bible, spiritual books, and even consolation from friends gave little relief.

Something had to change. I took out extra loan money and entered therapy.

One of my TA's referred me to Anita Sorenson, a Christian psychologist who gave Fuller students a discount. I showed up at her office hopeful but nervous. Even though I was studying to be a shrink, I'd never visited one before. I didn't know what to expect.

Anita opened the door and welcomed me inside. The first thing I noticed was how tall she was. It wasn't some psychological projection of a powerful mother figure either. The woman is over six feet tall.

She asked me why I was there.

"I have a lot of anxiety," I said. "Mostly about girls, but about other things too. Plus, I'm aggravated with my faith. It doesn't seem like I fit very well with Christianity anymore."

She just looked at me, waiting for me to continue. I decided to give her a little test.

"All the Christians at Fuller are hokey and legalistic and it drives me crazy," I said. Only that's not what I really said. I inserted two cuss words and one was the f-bomb. I knew that Anita was a Fuller grad, so I wanted to see if she could handle me uncensored.

Anita just sat there, waiting.

"Okay," I said. "I guess I'll talk some more. I'm sick of worrying about what everyone thinks, so it's like I try to make them mad on purpose."

"You look and sound like a teenager," she said.

"What? Because I swear?"

"No," she said. "It's your facial expressions and tone of voice. You roll your eyes a lot. I think that must be pretty hard for you."

"What do you mean?"

"It's not fun feeling like a teenager. You don't feel like you have any real control, but you want more from life and it makes you angry. You have a sense of what you're capable of, but you still feel afraid. That's what most teenagers sound like. That's what you sound like."

Whoa. Okay. This lady was scary, but in a good way. In exactly the way that I needed. I started seeing her once a week.

Anita never seemed put off by tales of my hedonism. She wasn't judgmental, but she didn't let me con her either. My quick wit, charm, and cynicism left her unfazed. She would only respond to what we later called my " backstage softness," emotions of sadness, love, and hurt. She helped me to delve into my anxiety instead of fighting it. We started finding answers for some of my problems, though we had a long road ahead of us.

The rest of 1994 was more stable. I began a Bible study with like-minded friends and we began, in Ryan's words, "trying to feel good about God again." My spiritual life was resuscitated, if not exactly healthy. Though I didn't grow much during this time, my anxiety was contained for a while.

I had no idea how much worse things would become.

. . .

At the end of my second year, I began pursuing with a vengeance a woman named Denise. She'd been my friend since the beginning of Fuller. I felt more relaxed around her than I did most women and we had a lot of similar interests. We had gone out a few times my first year, but nothing had come of it. We'd been spending more time together during my second year, so I thought it a natural transition for us to begin dating.

I asked her out to dinner a few times, but she always tried to minimize it. I'd ask her out for Italian and she would suggest we just go to Del Taco. We'd be goofing around and I would try to hold her hand, but she always made some kind of joke and pulled away. All this did was make me crazy. Denise and I spent hours together. She told me she thought I was a good-looking, funny guy and she didn't understand why I didn't have a girlfriend.

So why don't you do something about it? I'd think but never say.

I commiserated with friends, telling them that I was in love with her. Those closest to Denise always said, "You guys need to talk about this," but never gave me any encouragement.

By this time, Ryan and I had moved into a house with another friend of ours. One day, I was hanging out in Ryan's room, whining about my feelings for Denise. He was staring at his computer screen and didn't seem to be listening.

"I should say something to Denise about how I feel, but I don't want her to freak out."

"Then why don't you do something about it and shut up!" shouted Ryan. It totally caught me off guard. Ryan is a very laid back guy, and this was the first time I'd seen him mad, much less at me. It crossed my mind that I'd taken advantage of his willingness to listen. But it only crossed my mind. My feelings were hurt, but I didn't want to show him. I scowled, tossed two words at him, and walked out of the house.

I walked three blocks to Denise's apartment. I knocked and she opened the door.

"Ryan's a jerk," I said. "You want to go to Barnes and Noble or something?"

She gave me a hug and said, "Sounds perfect."

I picked up a copy of *Leaves of Grass* by Walt Whitman. We left the store, and I started reading "The Body Electric" to her as we walked down Colorado Boulevard.

"We need to talk," she said.

"Okay. What's up?"

"Not now. Let's get some beer and go back to my place."

"Beer on a school night?" I said.

"We're going to need it," she said. "At least I will."

We went to her apartment and settled in on the couch. My heart started beating faster as I anticipated what was coming. I assumed we were about to have a "DTR"—Defining Talk of the Relationship. I was right, but it was nothing like I imagined.

Denise took a deep breath and began.

"I know you think we should give dating a shot."

I shrugged, acting nonplussed as my pulse hit triple digits.

"Sure," I said. "Why not?"

"Steve, you know my friend Sophie, the one from Tulsa who visits me all the time?"

"Yeah, I know. She doesn't seem to like me very much. What about her?"

"We're more than friends."

I understood immediately. A million details about Denise and Sophie came into focus. Everything made sense in an instant. Something deep inside cried out in anger, but I punched it down.

We sat on the couch for a few seconds in silence. Then I stood up and said, "Come here."

I gave her a hug. I had just enough strength left to honor the fact that it had been difficult for her to tell me.

"I didn't expect this," she said. Without a word, I kissed her on the cheek and left.

I came unglued. I began drinking and smoking like a rock star. I no longer experienced the fever pitch of anxiety, but a morass of depression I hadn't felt since Bill died. Love and peace were unattainable in a world where a woman who seemed like such a good match didn't want me just because I was a man. I stopped talking to God. The Lord had created such a world and left me here alone.

Rock bottom came on the evening of May 15, 1995, two days after Denise had told me that she was a lesbian. I went to a party where Denise turned up with her girlfriend. I got drunk and sat in corner all night being quiet and sullen. When I returned home, I lay on the sofa and stared at the ceiling. Self-pity took the wheel and I became pathetic with melancholy. I didn't want to commit suicide, but I wanted it all to end. I told God so. What was left when nobody I really wanted to love me would? I told God that he needed to do something or just let me go to sleep and never wake up.

To my complete surprise, God did something.

As I drifted off in my stupor, I felt a hand on my shoulder, rousing me. I rolled over and saw Ryan. He said he was worried about me. He said he was sorry we hadn't been getting along lately.

"It's no big deal," I said. I was still soaking in self-pity, and playing the martyr felt more gratifying than dumping out all my woes.

Ryan sat down. "I would have been there for you, but I've been going through a lot lately."

I looked up at him sharply. Ryan doesn't wear his feelings on his sleeve like I do. I hadn't known he was going through anything. The only thing I had known was my own problems, my own obsessions. I sat up. "What's going on?" I asked.

Ryan told me about feeling lost and hopeless sometimes, just like me. He shared struggles that sounded so similar to mine, but my head had been too far up my melancholic behind for me to notice.

I shook my head. "This is amazing."

"What?" he said.

"I think God must have told you to wake me up. I needed this, man."

He laughed. We were in seminary, but we weren't usually that cheesy.

"No, really. I needed to see beyond myself. And I'm going to be here for you now. You can count on me."

He nodded. "Same here. Let me know whenever you need something."

I was suddenly a part of a community again, giving instead of only taking. For the first time in a very long time, I felt hope.

Ryan left, and I talked to God again. It was the second time in one night, after months of giving him the cold shoulder. "Thanks for sending Ryan," I said to him. "I may rethink this whole existentialism thing." Not the most suave opening, but I was still feeling ambivalent about faith and how God worked in the world. This was as good as it could get for now.

I'd wanted to die that night, and in a way I did. God let a little part of me die so that he could resurrect the rest.

• • •

On Ash Wednesday, 1996, I went to church for the first time in over a year. I sat in the back row alone.

"I'm sorry for running from you," I silently whispered to God.

No ray of sunlight fell on me to prove God's favor. Instead, I felt the full weight of my sin more heavily than before. I was ashamed of my blatant disregard for my relationship with Christ in favor of all my fruitless pursuits. I got goose bumps on my forearm as I felt the presence of God.

"I'm sorry," my heart said. "I'm so sorry."

I sat in the church for a long time after the service was over. For the first time in my life, I let myself feel pain and guilt. I almost willed it. I did not want cheap grace. I didn't want to ask forgiveness and move on. I had let my life and my heart stray far from my first love. I had tried to replace that love with partying, a girlfriend, and even anger. I had been chasing shadows when what I needed was the light. I was sick of walking in darkness.

I was energized. I wanted to do something. I wanted a concrete symbol of change. I wanted discipline in my life again. Not legalism, but a tangible practice that demonstrated my desire to get closer to God. I decided to give up alcohol for Lent.

Not drinking was easier than I thought it would be. It felt so wonderful to have an active relationship with God again that I didn't miss the booze. That Lenten season was a tremendous time of spiritual renewal. It culminated with a Good Friday service that made me feel the full weight of sin and grace all at once. I stayed in the church for almost an hour after the service, sitting alone with God. My salvation was exciting again.

In addition to my spiritual transformation, I began renewing myself physically. I had gained about thirty pounds since starting Fuller. My (literal) beer belly had become formidable, and gone was the athleticism of my early twenties. Extreme measures were called for, so I started training for a marathon. In a few months I dropped those thirty pounds and then some. I felt more myself in body, mind, and spirit.

A friend tried to get me to go out on a double date with him. "Sorry, pal. I've kissed dating good-bye. At least for a while."

He said, "I can see giving up booze for Lent, but women?"

I laughed. "I'm not giving up women for Lent. I'm just tired of the constant pursuit of a relationship in order to feel better about myself. I'm quitting the search for Mrs. Simpson." I was feeling content and peaceful for the first time in years and didn't want to muck that up by chasing some woman around.

I even found a church that didn't make me want to pull my hair out. I started attending a Mennonite church on the recommendation of friends who'd felt similarly disillusioned with church. The services challenged and convicted me without any of the legalistic nonsense that drove me nuts. I discovered that the greatest challenge before me was not to try to rein in my behavior, but to love as Christ did. I discovered that, despite all my blowhard pontification about the importance of love and grace over legalism, I had a lot of work to do in *really* showing love and grace to others. I had to admit that I was a selfish jerk.

In less than a year, God had restored me. He'd brought me back into his presence and made me whole. He reminded me how it felt to depend on him. He showed me, one more time, that cynicism doesn't really keep me safe — it just keeps me from joy. So I got to walk on the mountaintop with Christ for a little while, high above all that had once pained me. But you know how it goes. You can't stay up there. God doesn't give us spiritual highs to escape life; he provides them to prepare us for it. Soon it would be time for me to return to the valley. There was someone down there that God wanted me to meet.

5

Room
for Love

SHE'S TOO GOOD-LOOKING FOR ME, I THOUGHT. A WOMAN *that gorgeous would give me a conniption fit.*

It was my fourth year at Fuller Theological Seminary, and I was at my last required research seminar.

I have no memory whatsoever about the topic. All I remember is the unthinkably hot woman sitting in the second row. I could tell she was a first year by her eager, enthusiastic posture. She didn't have the hollow, resigned stare of an upperclassman like me. I stared at her for an hour, and it's really hard for me to focus on anything for that long. But staring is all I did because she was out of my league. I don't mean that I wasn't good enough for her; I just knew that talking to a woman that beautiful would bring me near panic. I had been enjoying life without anxiety for over a year, and I was in no mood to ruin that.

Six months later, on a sunny day in March, a buddy of mine asked if I wanted to play a quick game of spades. I had an hour before my next class, so I agreed. We walked together toward a bench in Travis courtyard. Two women sat there smiling at us. When I saw the one on the left, my stomach did a back flip. It was the beautiful woman from the research seminar. Closer inspection confirmed what I had known six months before — she was definitely out of my league.

"Steve, this is Shelley," my friend said.

"Hi!" she said and smiled.

"Hey," I said and didn't. I had on sunglasses and gave her the too-cool-for-school nod. She told me later that she knew I found her attractive in that second. She said that a guy doesn't try so hard to act cool unless he thinks you're cute.

Out of nowhere, another guy bounded into our foursome.

"Hey!" he said. "You guys playing spades? Can I play?"

"I'm sorry. We already have four," Shelley said.

"It's okay," I said. "I don't have time to play a full game anyway. You go ahead." The interloper pounced into my seat. I turned tail and fled.

A few weeks later, I was on my way to a U2 concert in San Diego with some friends. They were talking about some women from the first-year class who were going to meet us there. They seemed particularly excited about one named Shelley. I perked up when I heard her name, but shouted down any hopeful feelings. Apparently, a lot of guys were interested in her, and I wasn't about to subject my anxiety-prone psyche to competition for the affection of a lady. The fact that we were going to a U2 concert also helped to distract me. U2 meant far more to me than this Shelley person, no matter how cute she was.

My ticket put me in the seat next to Shelley's. I would've been excited about this if it weren't for the dude sitting on the other side of her. He had his arm around her chair in a not-so-subtle suggestion that he wanted it around her shoulders. I didn't know how to read this, but I didn't want to get in the middle of anything. Other than a polite greeting, I didn't talk to her until I had to.

"Do you mind if I smoke?" I asked.

For the first and last time, Shelley said, "No, go right ahead."

Then she started asking me questions. I answered and asked her some. Within minutes, I was having one of the best conversations of my life. We talked about God, music, sports, and life in graduate school. I remember laughing a lot. When I told her that I liked to run, she said we should go together sometime. Then the concert started, bringing a loud halt to our conversation. We promised to talk later and proceeded to rock and roll. It was, after all, U2.

Over the next few days, I thought a lot about Shelley but decided not to pursue anything. She'd had some guy's arm snaked around her chair; and every other guy I knew was drooling over her. I wasn't going to get my hopes up.

Then she called. "Hey, do you want to go run?"

Does a one-legged duck swim in circles?

Our relationship began with leisurely runs through the tree-lined streets of Pasadena. We ran slowly so we could talk. Sometimes one of us would start laughing so much that we had to stop. It was the best beginning to a relationship I've ever had. This wasn't some tension-filled process of mate selection thinly veiled as polite conversation over a froth-covered, over-priced caffeinated beverage. This was laughing and running with a beautiful girl. I was having the time of my life ... until I realized that I wanted to be her boyfriend and lost my mind.

It happened at the end of one of our runs. She was standing on the stairs to her apartment building, about to go in.

"Hey, what are you doing tonight?" I asked. I was praying to God in heaven that she would assume the sweat trickling in my eyes was solely due to the running and that my heart was jumping out of my chest because of the workout alone.

"I don't know," she said. *What was that supposed to mean? Yes or no?*

"Do you want to rent a video or something?" I asked.

She paused on the stairs, looking at her feet. She was thinking. As I waited a million years for her answer, I was sure she was thinking that we were not right for each other. I was edgy and sarcastic. She was sweet and graceful. I thought I might be too worldly for her, and she too naïve for me. Plus, every guy at Fuller without a ring on his finger had an eye on Shelley. Male seminarians circled Shelley like they were sharks and she was a wounded seal. My odds didn't look good. So why in the heck did I just ask her to watch a movie with me?

"Sure," she said.

Adrenaline surged through my veins, my heart rate doubled, and it's possible that I wet my pants a little. I dashed off to rent a movie. *Jerry Maguire* was in the new releases section. I hadn't seen it but heard it was good—something to do with sports. With no idea what I was getting myself into, I grabbed it off the shelf.

Let me tell you something about that *Jerry Maguire* movie— it's a great big scam. It starts off like a sports movie but quickly devolves into a romantic comedy. So there I am at eight o'clock on a school night, sitting on the couch next to a breathtaking woman, watching a love story masquerading as a sports movie. We were sitting close, not like two running buddies killing time. And that stupid movie was too close to reality. There's the loud-mouthed, worldly, ambitious guy falling for the sweet, gentle woman who will bring balance to his life.

I had no idea how to handle this situation. I couldn't play it cool or aloof. It's hard to act like nothing is happening when you're sitting on the couch next to a beautiful woman of amazing character watching Jerry stinkin' Maguire. There was no alcohol to lower my inhibitions. I couldn't show off or be funny while watching a movie. I had to sit there and accept the awful, exhilarating realization that I was gaga about Shelley.

When the movie was over, I wanted to kiss her good-night. We lingered in her doorway, drawing out the conversation. I hadn't the faintest clue how she would react, and I didn't want to blow things by moving in too early. I chickened out and went home, berating myself for not having the guts to give it a shot.

The next day I got up early because I couldn't sleep. I called Shelley. Her phone was busy, so I jumped in my car and drove to her apartment. I had a feeling that I couldn't contain, an impulse more pure than anything I'd ever felt for a woman. I don't mean holy or noble, just uncomplicated. I liked this woman a lot and nothing obscured that emotion, no second-guessing, no cynical dismissals, or even hesitancy due to fear of rejection. I needed to tell this woman how I felt, and nothing was going to stop that … except for another guy.

When I got to Shelley's apartment, she was on the phone with another one of her suitors. Since I'd been dialing her number over and over again like I was on crack, I knew she'd been on the phone with him for over an hour. The fire in my veins cooled, and hope went out for a coffee break. I excused myself and went down the hall to the apartment of one of my friends. He was home and let me in.

"I can't believe this," I told him, unable to hide my neurosis even from another dude. "I've totally got a crush on Shelley."

My friend's sympathetic demeanor turned cold.

"A lot of guys have crushes on her," he said flatly. "I get the feeling she's keeping her options open."

Oh, crap. He had a crush on her too. No safe quarry there, so I made casual conversation for a few minutes before finding an excuse to leave. When I got home, I started dialing her number again. I didn't care if Shelley had lunch scheduled with Brad Pitt and dinner and dancing with George Clooney. I had to tell her how I felt because this wasn't something I could sit on. I knew how to play all the games, how to be cool and move in sideways. But I didn't want to anymore. I was tired of trying to keep my passionate nature in check with everything from booze to running to cynicism.

Right before my fingers started bleeding from obsessive dialing, Shelley picked up.

"This might freak you out," I said. "But I felt something different last night. I think I really like you. I don't know what it means, and I don't expect you to do or say anything, but I was about to go crazy last night. I even wanted to kiss you."

Silence on the other end of the phone. No more than a couple of seconds passed, but it felt like three hours in a dentist's chair.

"I would have kissed you back," she said.

I smiled, and something relaxed inside my stomach. Cue the "Hallelujah Chorus," maestro.

• • •

Sounds like a happy ending, doesn't it? Well, yes and no. Dating Shelley was incredible—far better than any relationship that came before. But my anxiety came back with a vengeance. Something was different this time, however. Unlike other women who pulled away, Shelley drew closer to me during those times I feared her leaving. And that is precisely the thing that has made those fears vanish.

But first I had to confront some of the ways I conducted myself with women in the past. I had a pretty benevolent attitude about my sins with women, seeing my habit of indiscriminate kissing as some sort of Taoist, misguided good intention. With Shelley, I had to swallow the hard truth that I did a lot of really selfish, sinful, and ugly things. I'm not sure which is harder: trying to love things about yourself that once brought you shame or confronting the sinfulness of things which you once thought were no big deal. I went through some discouraging and disorienting times reconciling the things I used to do with the way I wanted to be with Shelley.

I discovered that being in a relationship and keeping it healthy is harder work than trying to get one in the first place. My selfishness became more apparent the longer Shelley and I were together. Learning to think of someone other than myself on a daily basis was a challenge. I had a hard time believing that the things I did and said had an impact on her. I had to learn to communicate, listen, and never take things for granted.

It kind of reminds me of that other big relationship in my life.

For all our talk about having a "relationship with God," Christians seldom treat it like an actual relationship. We don't express our feelings to God when we're angry or frustrated. We fear his wrath and flee from him when we think his designs might harm us. We pay tribute without drawing near. Though God is our sovereign Lord, we have an intimate relationship with him. Though I'd been a Christian for years, I hadn't really treated God like someone who loved me. I thought his love was distant and impersonal, something spread out across humanity. I couldn't believe that he suffered when I suffered. That's why I turned my back on him when my life got confusing and scary. I thought he didn't care anymore. I thought that, since I was a Christian, I didn't have to work at our relationship. I was behaving like a passive recipient of the edicts of a distant king. It never occurred to me that ignoring God was the thing creating my despair. Instead, I blamed it on him. But once I started talking to God again and nurturing our relationship, my feelings of despair evaporated. I discovered that griping about God does nothing. Griping *to* God invites him into the conversation.

And once he starts talking, it's hard to stay hopeless.

. . .

In the autumn of 2000, Shelley and I were driving up Foothill Boulevard in La Crescenta, California, looking for St. Luke's of the Mountains Anglican Church. At last, we saw it through a break in the trees—a small church built of gray stone and surrounded by flowers. It looked like something out of a Robert Frost poem.

"Rachel was right," said Shelley. "It's a really cute church. But I'd feel bad about asking the pastor to get married there since we don't attend."

"We could give it a try," I said. "It's not like we have our own church yet." Every church I liked was too liberal for Shelley, and every church Shelley liked was too conservative for me, if not just too loud. There was no harm in trying out one more.

We went to St. Luke's the following Sunday. It felt like God designed a worship service just for Shelley and me. Half the music was traditional, while the other half was praise and worship. There was both liturgy and unstructured time for public prayer. And Father Ron Jackson's sermon was perfect, encouraging a passion for Jesus Christ that left me feeling convicted but not browbeaten.

After the service, Shelley and I looked at each other and smiled.

"We might have found a church," I said.

"I hope so," Shelley said, smiling. "I wonder how friendly the congregation is?" She said this because nobody at our current church seemed to notice we were there.

"Hello!" said a voice behind us.

We looked to see a tall, blond, balding man in a white robe. It was Father Ron.

"I'm Ron Jackson, the pastor here," he said, shaking our hands.

Shelley and I introduced ourselves. Thirty minutes later, we were sitting on Father Ron's back porch drinking iced tea and talking. I hadn't felt like talking to a member of the clergy in years. He told us about the church and asked questions about our lives. He invited us to visit a new members' class. We agreed to attend on the spot.

"Um, by the way," I said on the way out. "We just got engaged a couple months ago. We might need a place to get married and someone to marry us."

Father Ron laughed. "You have no idea how many find us because they think the church would be 'a cute place to get married.' The only thing that's more surprising is how many of them join."

"After attending the service and talking to you," said Shelley, "I wouldn't be surprised at all."

We had a church home. It felt like the final piece of the puzzle. I had graduated a year before and was now a licensed Clinical Psychologist. Shelley was finishing her dissertation and was well on her way to graduating. I'd found a job as Clinical Director at Fuller Psychological and Family Services. Yes, I worked at Fuller. I even taught classes and saw clients there. In the very place I'd despised five years before. And I enjoyed it. More than a few people got a good laugh out of that one.

Shelley and I got married at St. Luke's in April 2001. A year later, we found a nice townhouse in Sierra Madre that we could afford. We brought home an affectionate and lively Golden Retriever/Cocker Spaniel mix from the pound and named her Sadie. I started working on a book, a dream that I'd deferred for too long as I struggled to bring order to my world. For the first time ever, it felt like my life was under control and I was free to pursue my passions.

The best part, however, was Shelley.

I started to gain some weight after we got married, which made me feel rotten. Because of my experiences in high school, my self-esteem became tied to how well my pants fit.

"I'm getting fat," I told her one day as I realized some old jeans no longer fit.

"That's one of the dumbest things I ever heard," she said. "You look better now than when we were dating."

"You're on drugs," I shot back.

She sighed. "One of these days, maybe you'll think as much of yourself as I do."

Things like this happened all the time. Whenever I started moping about some supposed flaw, Shelley not only told me there was no flaw, she said that she adored the very thing I despised about myself. From my hair looking like a static electricity experiment in the morning to my weird habit of rolling my tongue over my top lip when I look in the mirror, Shelley told me that the things I thought were embarrassing were actually cute.

In many ways, Shelley made me a better man. While I'm impulsive and easily bored, Shelley is steady and prudent. Where I'm sarcastic and indirect with affection, Shelley pours out love generously. She also has an uncomplicated passion for God that makes mine look dysfunctional and melodramatic. I found in Shelley things that were so hard to find in myself. Of course, this became a recipe for conflict sometimes, but it also helped me grow. Shelley did not complete me, but she inspired me. She called out strengths I didn't know were there. And she gave me a kind of love I'd never known before.

I was still a bit too wild for Shelley sometimes, but I was no longer in a reckless rage. My cynicism, though alive and well, no longer dominated my personality. I couldn't remain aloof and angry while faced with the reality of God's love. I'd fought a long and terrible war from which I emerged scarred but victorious. I had seen and done awful things, but God had countered them with meaning and beauty that pierced my heart with gladness. He'd sent people into my life as emissaries of his love and grace to prove that I wasn't alone and unlovable. I discovered that nothing melts cynicism faster than love, because that's what the cynic needs most. He needs someone to show him that it's okay to be vulnerable and trust. He must discover that there is healing for his broken heart, if only he will let someone in. When I let God in, he cleared out some space to make room for Shelley. At long last, I felt at peace.

Nobody told me the whole thing had just been a training exercise. God was just getting warmed up.

6

One, Two, Three ... Four?!

DR. BRUNDAGE'S FACE WAS A COLOR I'D NEVER SEEN before, something between dirty poodle white and dead canary yellow. He leaned back in his chair and put his hand over his mouth. I looked at the ultrasound monitor again. The three pulsing circles were still there.

"Do I see what I think I see?" I said.

"What do you see?" Dr. Brundage asked, his eyes never leaving the monitor.

"It looks like three."

"Actually, there's another one up in the corner. I think it's four."

Shelley jerked up from the examining table. "What?" she shouted. "You've gotta be kidding me!"

Dr. Brundage called in his wife, Linda, a veteran obstetrics nurse. She gazed into the monitor, the only one who didn't look ready to pass out or vomit.

"Yep," she said. "That's four."

Shelley was only five weeks into the pregnancy. She'd come in for an ultrasound because her hormone levels were unusually high, sometimes the sign of an ectopic pregnancy that would miscarry. Shelley had already suffered two miscarriages, so we arrived at Dr. Brundage's office steeling ourselves for the worst. Two miscarriages in less than a year had left us in a depressed stupor. I didn't know how we would survive a third. After the second miscarriage, we bought another dog to ease the pain. What was I supposed to do if Shelley lost another baby? Buy her a Shetland pony? Another failed pregnancy would be nothing less than devastating.

After the second miscarriage, Dr. Brundage prescribed Shelley the lowest dose of a drug called Clomid. It's designed to regulate ovulation cycles. According to research, the incidence of twins is only slightly higher on Clomid. When Dr. B gave Shelley the prescription, he said, "Don't worry, this doesn't give you litters of kids." Famous last words.

We had begged God for a child. Friends and family all over the world were praying for us. Patti Jackson, the wife of our pastor and mother of twins, said she was praying for "babies, plural." I thought nothing of it at the time (though all prayer requests go directly to her now). After all this praying, pleading and pestering, it seems that God's response was:

"All right, already! They want kids so bad? Quadruplets will shut them up."

Instead of facing another miscarriage, we were staring at an ultrasound screen with four little circles. Four little globes of life that flipped ours upside down. As we left the office, the staff didn't know what to do with us. There was a lot of awkward laughter, sighing, and head shaking. We shuffled out of the office in a fog, reeling from this surreal blow to our lives.

. . .

It hadn't been an easy year. After one of the miscarriages, Shelley had to endure a "D and C" procedure where they surgically removed the remains from her uterus. She no longer enjoyed the news of friends' pregnancies, and she loathed the sight of mothers with newborns. We skipped church a few times so Shelley wouldn't have to be around our pregnant friends.

After the second miscarriage, we got our second dog, Bella, which made things a bit more bearable, sublimating Shelley's maternal desires. Bella, a Shih Tzu–Pekingese mix, looks and acts like a clown. She's not the brightest dog in the world and she barks whenever the wind blows, but she gushes innocent affection. That lightened the darkness for a while.

Next, my career started hitting ridiculous roadblocks. I was getting turned down for jobs for which I was exceptionally qualified and had personal connections. Shelley had a new job that was going well, but the miscarriages made her miserable, and I felt like there was nothing I could do to help. During the summer of 2004, our lives were like a PG-rated version of the book of Job. We were certain that we'd break out in boils any second.

Then, in October, we found out Shelley was pregnant with quadruplets.

. . .

It would have been nice to celebrate, to rejoice at the prospect of an instant family. I wish we could have embraced God's gift of abundance in contrast to our previous losses. But we couldn't.

Too many things worried us. For starters, Shelley was only five weeks pregnant, and there was a chance that some of the embryos wouldn't survive. Other problems could result if all four babies made it to delivery. The babies would likely be premature and at-risk for a myriad of birth defects. It wasn't uncommon with quadruplets for one or more to die after they were born. Celebration was out of the question.

Then there was the other problem — me. None of my friends or family would pick me for the job of Quadruplet Dad. I definitely wouldn't. That night, I had a long talk with God.

God, I'm not your guy for this. I lose it when our dogs are acting up. Do you honestly think that me, the spoiled kid who's stingy with his time and space, is cut out to be a father times four? If you do, you're mistaken, or you know something about me that no one else does, including me. I can't do this. You're gonna have to give me something extra. A lot extra. I'm scared to death. This is the end of the life I know and want. It took a lot for me to get my head around having one child. How on earth do you think I'm the guy to be the father of four babies at once? Have you lost your divine marbles?

I didn't understand why God had put my wife and unborn children in a dangerous situation only to be met with a moody, fidgety father if they survived. In my darkest imaginings, I thought that one of the babies would probably miscarry, though that's the last thing I wanted. I could conceive of more loss, but not a script that features Steve in the role of Quadruplet Baby Daddy.

Shelley and I spent a lot of time consoling each other and talking through options and possibilities. I lost interest in work, and we spent a lot of time sleeping. Beneath it all, there was this hum of hopelessness, a feeling that there was no way this could end well.

As we arrived for our next appointment, we thought the situation couldn't become any more confusing or the stakes any higher. That's when Dr. Brundage introduced us to two words that tested us beyond anything we imagined: selective reduction.

"Selective reduction" is a euphemism for aborting one or more fetuses in a multiple pregnancy. We could tell from his face that Dr. B didn't enjoy bringing it up, but it was part of his professional duty. A quadruplet pregnancy is high-risk for the mother and babies. Reducing from quadruplets to triplets would decrease the probability of complications and increase chances of survival for the remaining three. Dr. B didn't outright recommend selective reduction, but he told us that the procedure was common in cases with more than three embryos.

"No way," was the first thing Shelley said to Dr. Brundage, and I shook my head in adamant agreement. Not only were we pro-life in principle, but also we couldn't stand the idea of aborting one of our kids. Dr. Brundage told us to take some time to think about it. He said we might want to do some research on the risks involved with a quadruplet pregnancy before we made a final decision.

Shelley and I agreed and started trawling libraries and the Internet. That's when we discovered what was at stake.

Quadruplets have a 70 percent survival rate. If we aborted one, there would be little-to-no risk of losing the remaining three. There's also a 50 percent chance that one or all of them would have major neurological problems. I'm not just talking about blindness or mental retardation; the babies could have such severe problems that they would die soon after birth. That was bad enough, but the danger to Shelley terrified me. She would be at risk for diabetes and a slew of maladies that I can hardly pronounce. The medications required to help her carry so many babies might raise her blood pressure so much that she could experience heart failure.

Death.

We had no idea what to do. Do we sacrifice one child in order to save the other three? If we did and had three healthy babies, would we feel guilty for the rest of our lives? If we didn't reduce and some or all ended up dying or had severe disabilities, would we feel even worse? Would keeping the babies cause too much trauma to Shelley's body, even to the point of death? My wife and I both have Master's degrees in Theology and PhD's in Psychology, but in that moment our educations were useless. Nothing we'd learned prepared us for this decision.

I started reading. I looked at everything from medical journals to books on Christian ethics for guidance. Nothing helped, including the pro-life literature. It only talked about abortion in the case of someone who doesn't want children. I found nothing that discussed abortion in a case where someone *wants* children. If we decided to reduce, it would be because we were pro-life—"pro" meaning having my wife and as many kids as possible survive. Neither secular nor Christian literature addressed the moral complexities of the decision we had to make.

Next came the stories. At first, they were positive. We heard from a dozen people who knew someone who knew someone who had quadruplets. Each was a success story, an anecdote about faith resulting in joy. That gave us hope until we heard morose tales of things going wrong. We listened to heartbreaking stories of severe impairment and death, of newborns suffering and dying. Many stories concluded with hard-nosed advice. Some said we were fools if we didn't reduce. Others said we weren't trusting God if we did.

Over the next few weeks, we went nuts trying to make a choice. We did our best to comfort each other, but came no closer to a decision. We begged God to show us what to do. "This is the kind of decision you're supposed to make," I told him. "This is too hard for a punk like me." I wanted God to let us off the hook, to write something on the wall. We didn't sign up for this. We never thought that trying to have kids would result in impossible life-and-death decisions.

Since we didn't know what we were going to do, and since one or more of the kids might miscarry, we only told those closest to us. My dad just kept saying, "I can't imagine being in your situation," and my mother promised to pray for us. My sisters, Suzanne and Lisa, called with words of support and encouragement but didn't tell us what to do. My college buddy Mark promised to pray for us and to crank call anyone who criticized us for whatever decision we made. Ryan and his new girlfriend Jen promised that they would stand by us whatever happened, though Ryan seemed almost as dumbfounded as I was by the whole thing.

Everyone prayed, listened, and loved us, but they didn't tell us what to do. There was a hazy buffer between us and the rest of the world. It felt like everyone was standing one step away, kind of like they were at the snake exhibit at the zoo. They didn't mind being nearby, but they didn't want to tap on the glass and shake things up. They wanted to be close without affecting our decision. I don't blame them. Even if someone had an answer to this impossible question, why would they want that kind of responsibility?

Shelley expressed her pain through tears. I released angry spew into my journal. We came no closer to a decision, asking God repeatedly why he had put us in this ludicrous situation.

Help finally came in the form of a man, not an answer. Dr. Ray Anderson, professor of Systematic Theology at Fuller Seminary where I teach, had been one of our favorite professors in grad school. He's one of those teachers who rattles the way you see the world. His lectures emanated from a place deeper than mere knowledge. He was once a farmer, and it was as if he summoned wisdom up from the ground. He stared down ethical dilemmas, encouraging his students to think about them from a divine perspective rather than offering pat answers. The guy even had a timeless glow about him. He looked no more than fifty-five, but he was at least a hundred and two, if you believe the rumors. When someone suggested that we talk to him, we felt silly for not thinking of it sooner.

We showed up at Ray's office on a Thursday afternoon when Shelly was ten weeks along. He welcomed us and asked us to sit on an old, academic-looking sofa.

"Quadruplets, eh?" he said, sounding like a little like Sean Connery in his post-Bond years. "That must have been quite a shock. How are the two of you holding up?"

Though we hadn't spoken with him in years, we poured out our hearts. He listened. He made sure that he understood our situation and feelings. Then he went to work.

Ray offered more wisdom than we'd found anywhere else. However, he didn't take away our pain, and he certainly didn't tell us what to do. He said that it was impossible for us to make the "right" decision. We could only make the best decision in a situation where there was no obvious choice. He told us that either choice involved potential guilt and loss. We might have to ask forgiveness from God regardless of what we chose. If we decided to reduce, we would have to ask forgiveness for taking a life. If we decided not to, and Shelley or the babies were harmed during the pregnancy, we might have to ask forgiveness for not reducing. And I knew that if Shelley didn't survive, I would be begging forgiveness for the rest of my life.

Ray said that facing this sort of decision is part of being a Christian, part of living responsibly in a fallen world. Nowhere in the Bible does God promise us a pain-free existence. He doesn't call us to a life of simple choices with predictable outcomes. But he does call us to be like Christ. Jesus had to make agonizing choices, and he was sometimes afraid. He even asked his Father to spare him the painful journey to the cross. To be like Christ doesn't mean an easy road. It often means making decisions that you know will result in suffering.

Whoopee.

But Ray also told us something else. "You're looking for answers," he said, "when what you need are accomplices."

Huh?

"No one can tell you what to do, but we can support you. What you need are people to shoulder the load with you." He stopped and looked at each of us for a moment. "I want to be your accomplice." It sounded like he was applying for a secret spy job or something. "And here's how I'll do it. Not only will I support whatever decision you make, you go ahead and tell other people that I'm in on it."

Though that felt very Christian, it felt very little like the institutional religion I'd grown up around. I was used to people covering their butts and distancing themselves from controversy. Now here was Ray, telling us that he was going to step into the breach with us, regardless of what it cost him. Shelley and I smiled at each other. It didn't feel like we were out of the woods yet, but at least we weren't in the woods alone.

Then we began to notice our other "accomplices." Each other, first of all. We also had our families, our friends, and our church. Even our dogs, Sadie and Bella, chilled out and became more affectionate than usual—maybe misery has its own scent.

Perhaps our biggest accomplice, however, was Shelley's grandmother, a fascinating and lovely woman. She was tender yet mischievous, stubborn yet compassionate. She was an artist and an intellectual. She had strong political opinions tempered by a gracious, listening heart. She was also the kind of diligent, ferocious prayer warrior that creates earthquakes in hell. She was, as much as anyone I've seen, the way that God wants us to be in this fallen, crazy world—whole. She had many different talents, traits and quirks, but she was always Mommo Gregg. You felt her powerful, playful, loving presence even when she was sitting near you in silence.

She prayed for us day and night and let us know about it. It was like sneaking an NBA player onto a JV basketball team. If the devil had any interest in this matter, Mommo Gregg would leave him no choice but to take his ball and go home.

In the midst of our hopelessness, people wrapped us in a warm cocoon of love. Nobody could tell us what to do because the decision was too big, but they could love us. I should have known. I practiced and preached the power of love over answers in my work as a psychologist. In psychotherapy, it seldom helps if I tell my clients what to do. Though most people come looking for answers, answers are not really what they need. They need someone to sit with them in their pain or walk with them through the darkness. They need collective courage in the face of pain and confusion. Not every situation in life has an easy answer, but it's easier to pass through those times if you don't have to walk alone.

Now, before you start thinking this is some testament to relativism, let me explain. I believe in Truth. I believe in right and wrong. I believe in testing things with Scripture and remaining obedient to God. But I'm not talking about moral dilemmas; I'm talking about suffering. When we're suffering, the best moral decision usually doesn't take away the pain. No physician, scientist, theologian, or pastor could tell us what to do. Even if someone gave us an answer with rock-solid logic, it wouldn't have taken away the fear. What kept us from despair were the accomplices holding our hands as we waded through the dark sludge of anxiety toward an impossible choice.

We had to decide before the twelfth week of pregnancy whether or not to reduce. After that, the procedure would be too risky. We went in for one more ultrasound before making our choice. What I saw on the screen almost killed me. Where before there had been four pulsing blobs, there were now four little babies. We could see tiny heads and tummies. Their heads were gigantic and they looked like they had tails, but they were beautiful and very much alive. They were moving, practically dancing. I had never seen anything more wonderful.

I felt like I was going to be sick. I had never expected to feel so much love for four little things that looked like aliens out of a bad sci-fi flick.

Our decision came at the eleventh hour, the evening before the deadline. Shelley lay in bed crying. I collapsed at the foot of the bed. "What do you want to do, honey?" I stared at the ceiling. "It's up to you. I'll support whatever you choose."

Intellectually, we knew that selective reduction made the most sense. After reading the research and weighing the possible outcomes, we understood it to be the safest choice. But Shelley said she could imagine going in for the procedure and then changing her mind and walking out. Safest choice or not, it felt like too much of a sacrifice.

"If it were up to me, I wouldn't reduce," Shelley said. Her tears had stopped, but she still had the little hiccups that come after a good cry. I was about to say that it was up to her, but then she quickly added, "That's not a firm decision."

We sat in silence for a moment, me still on the end of the bed with her feet pushed into my chest.

We each wanted the other to make the final choice and cast off the burden.

I rolled off the bed, left the room, and lumbered down the hall to my office. I went prone on the ground. With angry sobs soaking the carpet, I began to pray.

I might have to ask forgiveness for what we decide, Lord, but I'm also going to have to forgive you for putting us in this situation. I'm so mad at you, God. I need you to show up huge right now. I know I've asked you that before—asked for the immediate answer—for stupid things. But this isn't stupid. This is bigger than me. And I need you to show up right here, right now.

I felt something wet and cold on my neck. Sadie was licking me. Whenever one of us was upset, Sadie responded by soaking us with affection. I laughed and scratched her ears. I rolled over on my back and she climbed on top of me, staring me in the eye and slapping me with her tongue whenever I stopped petting her.

I went back into the bedroom. Shelley was trying in vain to sleep.

Okay, God, I said. *I trust you. I'm mad and I'm scared to death, but I know that you have a plan and a will for us. I'll make a decision. The rest is up to you.*

"I can't do it," I said. "I can't stand the thought of aborting one of our kids. I'd rather take a risk now and suffer later."

"Okay," she said in resignation. I kissed her, and she rolled over and fell asleep.

I didn't feel better, but at least we had made a decision. And, for the first time, it felt like I was in familiar territory. So far, I had been living as if I had to be cautious, weighing evidence to determine the safest option. It felt too defeatist, as if we had to safeguard against the worst-case scenario. As a cynic, I'd been playing it safe for years and I was tired of it. I wanted to have hope and expect great things. If nothing else, going for all four felt like something I would do.

When we told Dr. Brundage about our decision the next day, the man got a fire in his eyes.

"Yes," he said. "I don't know how anyone can make 'Sophie's choice.' That's too tough." He then proceeded to rattle off everything we were going to do to help these babies survive. He was a new man, passionate and driven. I liked what I was seeing. He concluded by telling Shelley, "If you can make it to thirty weeks, I'll give you four healthy babies." Now *that's* an accomplice.

We let the world know that Shelley was pregnant with quadruplets. We summoned armies of prayer warriors, and they responded with vigor. Friends told friends who told their friends. The next thing we knew, some lady in France we'd never met was sending us emails of prayer and support. Maybe those little dancing babies had a chance.

7

Puking and Eternity

AFTER WE DECIDED TO KEEP ALL THE BABIES, THE morass of depression lifted for a little while. We had a concrete goal: doing all we could to protect the pregnancy and Shelley's health. We were anxious but no longer dispirited. That lasted for about two weeks. Then began a time that made the previous summer look like a trip to Club Med.

It started with the puking. I don't mean garden-variety morning sickness. Shelley's vomiting was so bad that there's a special name for it: Hyperemesis Gravidarum. It's when someone throws up so much that it threatens her health. Ironically, it was a condition with which I was already well acquainted. As proof that God combines good planning with a sense of humor, my doctoral dissertation was on Hyperemesis. In my training as a psychologist, I "somehow" managed to do research on a rare pregnancy puking disorder.

The medical folklore on Hyperemesis is that it's a psychosomatic disorder—translation: it's all in the pregnant woman's head. If you mention this to a woman afflicted with Hyperemesis, you'll be lucky to get away with *your* head intact. The research I did revealed that the condition results not from psychological problems but from hormonal sensitivity. Because I'd done research on Hyperemesis, I was able to suggest a couple of things, like ginger root, that helped Shelley a little and me a lot—I didn't feel totally useless. But, more than anything, my knowledge about Hyperemesis gave me more sympathy and patience than I might have had otherwise. I need all the help I can get in this department.

Shelley spent the autumn of 2004 in and out of the hospital because her life was an uninterrupted nausea and vomiting festival. In her second trimester, she weighed less than she did before she was pregnant. Every couple of weeks, she'd head back to the hospital for another round of rehydrating intravenous meals and anti-vomiting medication.

Making matters worse, Shelley's grandmother, Mommo Gregg, had a stroke around Thanksgiving. It left her with impaired speech and, even though she possessed a fighting spirit, her health declined rapidly. Shelley wanted to be at her side all the time, but couldn't manage it while throwing up every ten minutes. When the doctors said that Mommo Gregg might not have long to live, it broke Shelley's heart that she couldn't be with her day and night.

Shelley kept up her spirits as best she could, but she was hard to console. She was always in pain and sometimes didn't even have the energy to talk. The one person who always made Shelley feel better, however, was her therapist, Randy Sorensen. Shelley and I are both psychologists and, if you want to be a halfway decent shrink, you need to get your own therapy. Not only does it help you address your own baggage, but also it teaches you how difficult it can be to be a client in therapy. Therapists' therapists are special. They're counselors and analysts but also mentors who help you figure out how human beings change and grow. It's a special, sacred relationship.

Shelley had been working with Randy for five years. Randy was married to my therapist, Anita. It happened more or less by coincidence. I was working with Anita before Shelley started with Randy. A friend had recommended Randy to Shelley, and he happened to have a spot open and agreed to a fee that we could afford. It felt a little strange, but we knew that Randy and Anita would abide by their ethical codes and not kibitz behind our backs. It had never been a problem. Randy had been a pillar of support and encouragement during her pregnancy, and we were both grateful for him.

Despite all her pain and puking, Shelley kept her head in the game. She ate all the right foods, even though they made her nauseated. She took all her medications and monitored her health diligently. She was determined to make this work.

Meanwhile, I was running scared.

I'm a good problem solver as long as I'm in my comfort zone, but Shelley's suffering was unfathomable for me. My usual tricks —being clever, cool, and funny—were useless. The only way I could help my wife was by doing something that I'm terrible at: sitting still. I could sit in an uncomfortable chair near her bed while she groaned, sweated, and watched a television without cable. I could reconcile Shelley's countless medical bills with insurance statements, which is pretty much the Ninth Circle of Hell for someone with Attention Deficit Disorder.

I felt powerless to do anything that could help, so I retreated. I spent most nights at our townhouse instead of driving across town to stay with Shelley at her parents' place. I could rationalize it because I was working a lot. We were going to need money, after all. I was taking on an extra job and preparing for our move into a new house that was more quadruplet-friendly than our Yuppie enclave. All this justified my withdrawal from that which I couldn't control. One time, however, God didn't let me escape. When Jonah was running, God tossed him into the belly of the whale. God snagged me with a Santa suit.

By Christmas, Mommo Gregg's health was failing, and we knew she didn't have long. The stroke had robbed most of her speech, and she was in a haze of confusion and pain much of the time. Shelley's mom Vickie got the notion that someone should visit her dressed as Santa Claus in order to lift her spirits. When she suggested that I do it, I balked. Though I can be a histrionic ham in the right situation, the idea of frolicking in front of a dying woman dressed as St. Nick was well beyond my comfort zone. What if I scared her? What if she was in too much pain for yuletide shenanigans? What if I gave her another stroke? She might think I was an intruder and call the police! So I told Vickie I'd think about it, hoping she'd forget and I'd be off the hook. But when we went to visit Mommo one December night, Vickie pulled a Santa outfit from the trunk of her car. She handed it to me and smiled. I'm pretty sure I heard God laugh and say, "You can run but you can't hide, Pal—especially from your mother-in-law."

I grudgingly put on the fuzzy red costume and stuffed a pillow under my shirt. I knew that I couldn't fake this. There's no such thing as a subdued Santa. So I got my jolly on and went to work.

Mommo Gregg lit up when she saw me. Her eyes came to life, and she started laughing. It was all the encouragement I needed. I put on a show, complete with "Ho Ho"-ing and tales of reindeer soiling her lawn. When I asked her if she'd been naughty or nice, she said, "A little nice." Not only were they the most words she'd spoken in days, but also they were classic, mischievous Mommo Gregg.

Thank God Vickie pushed me into doing it. God had a job for me to do, and he wasn't going to let me get away. I'm glad he didn't, because Mommo died a few days later. As if my poor wife wasn't suffering enough.

      ◆ ◆ ◆

Over the holidays, when Shelley was about three months along, she finally got some relief. She didn't feel as nauseated and she started gaining weight. That's when we made the mistake of going out to dinner on New Year's Eve.

We didn't go to some hole-in-the-wall diner, but to a place with white tablecloths, tuxedoed waiters, and a national reputation for great steaks. It was our first night out in a long time and we had a blast. The food was delicious—going down. Coming back up, not so much.

We both got food poisoning. It hit me first. I was wretching my lungs out at four o'clock on the first morning of 2005, but at least I got the foul urchin out of my system. Shelley, however, was on anti-emetic drugs that prevented her from throwing up. The nasty microscopic varmints got plenty of time to wreak havoc on her body. Her gastrointestinal system went haywire, and she started erupting like Mt. Vesuvius. A nasty virus called C. *diff* had infected her. She ended up in the hospital for over a week, trying to keep down rice and apple juice. She became anemic and needed oxygen and a series of EPO injections. She vomited around the clock, making endless trudging treks to the bathroom.

"You okay?" I asked when she came out of an especially long visit to the bathroom. I felt helpless, wishing I could do the puking for her.

She walked right past me, climbed into bed, and said, "At least I know I'll be in heaven one day."

Most of us have pleasant daydreams of the afterlife, but if you're like me, you don't think about it seriously. I usually consider heaven a luxurious retirement community where I'll eat saturated fats with my loved ones, run through the clouds with deceased pets, and play shuffleboard with golden pucks. I live as though the real rewards come in this life, even though I know better.

After weeks of being a human vomit machine, Shelley understood that heaven is the goal, not the bonus prize we get after finding peace on earth. She knew that there was no safe haven here. We can have periods of happiness, but most of it will be restlessness and struggle. Only in the eternal presence of God will we receive lasting peace. Some people have to reach old age to figure this out. Shelley figured it out at thirty, as she carried four babies without the satisfaction of nourishment.

In this life, the best we can hope for is an occasional reprieve from the struggle. But those reprieves count for something, and God gave us a good one while Shelley languished in the hospital. Dr. Marc Incerpi, our perinatologist and a saint of a physician, made a special trip to Shelley's room for an ultrasound. But this was no routine ultrasound. This one would reveal the genders of our kids.

When people asked us how many girls and how many boys

we wanted, we always said, "Four healthy babies." But secretly I told God, "At least one boy." Little girls are delightful and I would have been thrilled with a whole litter of them, but it would be nice to have another male swimming with me through the sea of estrogen. God answered me more literally than I had expected.

Dr. Incerpi found a boy first. Then a girl. Then another girl. Then another. Three girls and a boy! It was the first time I'd seen Shelley smile in days. Thinking of the creatures in her belly simply as the babies felt slightly impersonal. Now we had three little girls and a little guy we could dream about. We could imagine their faces. We could imagine our family.

* * *

When Shelley was released from the hospital, she moved out of our townhouse and in with her parents across town. She was on bed rest and needed constant care. I had to work and couldn't provide it, so Shelley moved in with her parents. One night in January, I called Shelley to tell her I was leaving work and on the way over. When I spoke with her on the phone, she was fine. When I walked into the door of her parents' house, she was bawling.

Before I could even ask what was wrong, she said, "Randy died."

My head went light. When I recovered, I went to comfort Shelley, though I was feeling numb and lost.

"What happened?"

Shelley managed to pause her crying to get the story out. "I tried calling him for our appointment" — she had been doing telephone conferences with her therapist ever since she went on bed rest — "and he didn't answer."

I nodded. That would be troubling. Randy didn't miss appointments. Randy had suffered some sort of attack a couple of hours before his appointment with Shelley. No one is sure what happened. While I'd been driving to her parents' house, one of Randy's colleagues had called Shelley to let her know.

"Oh, Shelley …"

"I can't believe he's gone!" And Shelley was crying again. Shelley needed Randy. He was sometimes the only one who could give Shelley hope during the pregnancy. And I couldn't imagine what his wife Anita was going through. I felt powerless to help, once again. My wife is a wreck, her therapist is dead, and my therapist has to deal with the loss of her husband. We were all in the middle of a cosmic meltdown. It felt like God had fallen asleep and let the universe go off the rails.

Just when Shelley needed Randy the most, God plucked him from her life. Shelley had lamented that her only relief would come in heaven; and her friend, counselor, and mentor had beaten her there. I had a few choice words for God in my journal that night, and I went to sleep mad at him.

It was too much. It felt like God had become one of the reckless gods of Greek mythology, twisting fate at his whim. Or maybe he just didn't care. Regardless, I could see no method to God's madness. I could think of no good reason for my wife to endure this trauma trifecta.

Through all this pain, however, God was teaching us a lesson. He was preparing us for something that we would experience over and over again: the blessed connection between joy and pain. Shelley wouldn't have been suffering if she didn't love our children. She wouldn't have felt overwhelming grief if Randy and Mommo hadn't brought her immeasurable joy. I wouldn't have been at the brink of insanity if I didn't love Shelley.

Love is a dangerous thing. It comes at a price. The relationships that bring us the most joy—whether with a friend, family, lover, or even God—also bear the most potential for pain. People die. Children leave. God's presence can be elusive. We suffer because we love, because we let others into our lives. It wasn't the death of Randy and Mommo that hurt—it was the stark contrast of life without them. The incredible joy they brought made things darker once they were gone. It couldn't have been any other way. While we walk on the earth, joy and love will bring pain. The two are inseparable. When pain precedes joy, the contrast makes the joy more potent. When joy precedes pain, the pain wakes you up to the wonder and depth of what you once had. It clears the distractions, annoyances, and self-preoccupation so you can focus on the amazing gift that God gave you.

I'd always told myself that I wanted to be like Jesus, but I don't think I really understood what that meant until Shelley got pregnant and the world started to collapse. Jesus loves us so much that he suffered and died for us. He loves us so much that his heart breaks when one of us turns away from him. The thing that brings us closest to the heart of God is risky love. It's accepting that the joy and love you feel now can cause your soul to ache later. Being like Christ means accepting that you can't have one without the other, and to have neither is to be spiritually dead.

Shelley figured this out while she was throwing up in the hospital. She understood that she wouldn't know lasting peace until the end. Maybe that's why she remained strong through all her tribulations. Maybe that's why she grew through the pain. I'm glad one of us did.

I was more frustrated with God than ever. More than when Jeff showed up at my church, more than when Bill died, and more than any time while I was in seminary. Before, the only thing at stake had been my faith and sense of purpose in the world. The stakes were much higher now. This time, my wife endured what seemed like senseless torment while her life and the lives of my children were at risk. Shelley might have been looking forward to heaven, but I was shouting at it.

One night during Shelley's sixth month, I stood alone on the balcony of our townhouse. My hand hung at my side, clutching a beer bottle by the neck. I looked up into the orange glow of the Southern California night sky as tears of frustration ran down my face.

"God," I said, "I need to see your hand, and I need to see it now. I'm not asking for strength or wisdom or grace or any of that stuff I'm supposed to pray for. It's time for you to throw down Old Testament style. It's miracle time. Will you please help?"

Despite my lack of faith, God said, "Yes."

8

Miracle
Drug

EVEN THOUGH SHELLEY WAS IN CONSTANT PAIN AND I was in constant panic, we started to feel more optimistic as the pregnancy approached seven months. Though miserable, Shelley was in good health, and the babies appeared to be developing well. We gave ourselves permission to get a little excited. Picking out names helped.

Hayley Rose
Ella Marie
Jordan Andrew
Emma Grace

I prayed for my children by name and imagined calling them by name. I pictured their faces and wondered about their feelings. It made me feel like I really had kids.

I loved them.

Shelley had entered the critical final weeks of her pregnancy. Multiple births are almost without exception premature. The longer the babies stay in the womb, the healthier they will be. The more premature they are, the more at risk they are. Every anxious day that Shelley went without going into labor or developing dangerously high blood pressure and forcing a delivery was a gift to the babies.

The anxiety I felt for my children was worse than any I'd ever felt, and I'm a pretty anxious dude. I couldn't focus at work. I started having a couple of beers at night so I could sleep. While Shelley stayed in bed, I ran for miles and miles, trying to wear out my feelings. I could imagine nothing worse than one of my children suffering, or, God forbid, dying. Actually, yes I could. The danger to Shelley petrified me. She was doing great and her physicians marveled, but danger still lurked: the risk of the surgery, her low iron levels, and the possibility of dangerously high blood pressure, just to name a few. I wanted my wife to be done with this. I wanted to hold my children, and I wanted them to be healthy. But I had to wait and worry, pestering God about the preposterous predicament we were in.

But God does little things to sustain us when he doesn't deliver the goods on the spot. When it's not time for the voice to come out of the whirlwind or the sea to part, he sprinkles four-leaf clovers of benevolence to keep us on our feet. He gave Moses water from the rock. He gave Joshua a horn to blow. He gave Samson some honey. He gave Gideon a wet fleece. During the spring of 2005, God gave me a U2 song.

Though I doubt Bono and God discuss the matter, U2 albums arrive right when I need them. The tone of the album and the words of the songs are always apropos to wherever I am in life. I know—I project a lot of what I need to hear onto nebulous lyrics. While Shelley was pregnant, U2 released a new album, *How to Dismantle an Atomic Bomb*. The second track was titled "Miracle Drug." The first verse made me ache to see my children, as it talked about the desire to get to know some-one from the inside out. It even mentioned a newborn baby.

It was perfect.

I wanted to touch, hear, and see my kids. I wanted them to hear my voice and know my love. I wanted freedom from all this anxiety and waiting. That freedom would only come when I could smell the tops of their newborn heads. Bono wrote "Miracle Drug" for someone in a far worse predicament, but I indulged in that first verse as I waited for my wife and children to be set free.

But there was another part of the song that foreshadowed what was about to happen.

> *I hear your voice, it's whispering ...*
> *I was a stranger you took me in.*

In Matthew 25:35, Jesus says, "For I was hungry and you gave me something to eat, I was thirsty and you gave me something to drink, I was a stranger and you invited me in." Immediate, divine rescue is awesome and sometimes necessary, but I don't think that's the way God prefers to work. I think he likes to work through his children. He allows dire situations that bring people together and bring out their absolute best. He creates circumstances that tap hidden resources of love, grace, strength, and knowledge. He uses desperation to make our gifts shine. I had been griping, moaning, and pleading for over a year because I wanted God to pull a rabbit out of a hat. But he had something much deeper and more potent in mind. Through science, medicine, friends, family, and love, God was about to perform a whopper of a miracle.

I was too freaked out to notice that God had set the stage perfectly. We had brilliant physicians and medical staff who were generous with their time and invigorated rather than daunted by a quadruplet pregnancy. Shelley's younger brother was finishing his pediatric residency and was an amazing resource. Though Shelley has a rare blood type, we found plenty of matches among family and friends who gladly donated blood in preparation for Shelley's surgery. The people of St. Luke's took the pregnancy as a rallying cry for prayer and community. Our pastor, Father Ron, made special trips to minister to us and give us communion when Shelley couldn't make it to church. The congregation showered us with donations and commitments to help with childcare. Shelley's parents had just retired and were available around the clock to care for her. They helped us in every way imaginable. My family, though they were on the other side of the continent in Kentucky, made us feel like they were next door with their constant prayer, love, and support.

Then there was Shelley. My wife is loving, kind, and compassionate. She's the most amazing woman I've ever known—and she's white-hot cute. She's also stubborn as a carpet stain and so detail-oriented that it makes me dizzy. If Nazis had tortured her with blunt instruments and polka music, it wouldn't have deterred her from the meticulous regimen she adopted in order to keep herself and the babies healthy. She was persnickety about eating nothing but the best food for the babies. She stayed on bed rest for eight months, lying only on her left side. She did everything the physicians told her to do—and more. She endured arthritis, back pain, poor circulation, galloping heart beat, breathing difficulties, and a bizarre skin lesion on her hand. She was dogged, determined, and obstinate in the face of constant discomfort and grounds for despair.

Shelley paid a price for her determination, however. She was confined to her bed and never left the house except to go the doctor. Her body was wracked with pain. Eating made her nauseated. Since she was under doctor's orders to consume enough calories to fly the Space Shuttle, she felt sick all the time. She couldn't do any of the things she loved, like walking our dogs or going out for iced coffee. She couldn't even sit in a chair and watch television. On top of all this, she lived under the constant threat of something going wrong with the pregnancy. Shelley survived a nightmare I can't even imagine.

The average term for a quadruplet pregnancy is twenty-nine weeks. My wife made it to thirty-three. She gave the babies a critical extra month to grow in the safety of her womb. She gave our children a gift that will benefit them for the rest of their lives. Though I had questions about God's judgment in picking me for this gig, God obviously knew what he was doing when he chose Shelley.

When we arrived at the hospital for the delivery, we showed up to a carnival. I think everyone who worked in Labor and Delivery showed up that day. Over twenty people bustled around the delivery room, each with a different job. People were chattering and laughing, giddy with anticipation. It was like a party where the guest of honor looks like she swallowed a beach ball.

I wasn't ready to have fun, however. I was scared. Shelley wasn't scared—she was done. She was in a dozen different types of pain and had difficulty breathing with the weight of four babies on her diaphragm. The pregnancy had been a marathon for her and this was mile twenty-five. She just wanted to cross the finish line and get it over with. I attempted to keep Shelley's spirits up by trying to make her laugh. The few times that I succeeded, she got mad at me because laughing hurt too much.

As they prepped her for the C-section, I put on surgical clothes, complete with mask, cap, and booties. I looked like a reject from a medical soap opera. Then they carted Shelley off to the operating room, and I was alone. Everyone who'd been cavorting around Labor and Delivery disappeared into the delivery room. Shelley's nurse confined me to a chair in the hallway and told me to wait. They would call me in just before they delivered the babies.

So I sat.

And waited.

In an antiseptic white hallway in dense silence.

I started praying. "God," I said. "You know how I feel and what I'm about to ask. So I'm not even sure — "

"Steve?" It was one of the nurses.

"Yeah?"

"You can come in now."

The double doors of the operating room swished open. Blipping, blinking contraptions with tubes coming out of them were everywhere. Four tiny beds were spread around the perimeter of the room. Three people attended each one. Half a dozen others surrounded the operating table. Linda Brundage was running around with a video camera. In the center of the room was Shelley, or rather, her torso. Her bottom half was concealed by a large sheet, which was fine by me. Behind the sheet, Dr. Brundage and Dr. Incerpi stood across from each other over Shelley's belly. Their arms moved behind the sheet, but I couldn't see their hands. It looked like they were playing a friendly game of foosball. The festival mood from the hallway persisted. Everyone was laughing and having a good time ... while my heart was about to explode.

I sat next to Shelley and stroked her hair. She stared at the ceiling with tired eyes, commending it all into God's hands.

The fun stopped and a hush fell. Everyone on the other side of the sheet looked toward Dr. Brundage and Dr. Incerpi's foosball game, which had become fast and frantic. The moment had arrived.

Dr. B suddenly looked worried and intent, like he was losing the foosball game. I later learned that, after he opened the amniotic sac, three of the babies had slipped on top of the fourth. Dr. B had to get the baby on the bottom first. Using forceps, he wrangled Hayley Rose free. When I heard her cry, my shoulders dropped and my breath released. Then came the beautiful scream of Ella, followed by Jordan. When Dr. B pulled out Emma, I heard nothing. They took her to her bed and started hooking things up to her. Still, I heard nothing.

Why isn't she crying? I thought. *What's the matter? Why don't they do something?*

"Waaaaaaa!" said Emma. *Why did the little rascal make me wait so long? Didn't she know that her father was a nervous wreck?*

Some emotions are too big to verbalize. We don't have names for them. They come from deep places in our hearts where words don't exist. I remember a lot about what happened in that delivery room. I remember beautiful, anxious, joyful, and disgusting details. But I still can't tell you what happened. Even the video fails to communicate it. After all of our fear, frustration, and suffering, our babies were born. I wish I could tell you how it felt, but I can't. The words that I love so much when I'm writing or teaching are useless in the face of what I felt when Hayley, Ella, Jordan, and Emma burst into the world. But I'll try to tell you some of what happened after.

First, I went into the waiting room to tell everyone what had happened. I swung open the door to see Shelley's mom, Vickie, and her father, Todd, along with a bunch of Shelley's aunts, uncles, and cousins. (My parents wouldn't arrive until the next day, saying, "You've got enough on your hands without worrying about us.") Everyone stood up. Vickie's eyes swelled with tears when she saw the smile on my face.

"Shelley is doing great," I said. "She gave birth to a poodle, a schnauzer, a terrier, and ..."

Todd chuckled, but everyone else just stared. *Wrong time for a joke. Steve's a dork. Move on.*

"Shelley is great, and the kids are all okay."

Everyone started cheering, crying, and hugging, but I didn't join in. I wanted to see my wife.

Shelley was fine—a heckuva lot smaller, and breathing easier without eighteen pounds of babies on her diaphragm. But, in what felt like a moment of complete injustice, they separated her from her children. They carted her off to be sewn up and put back together while the babies went to the Neonatal Intensive Care Unit (NICU). So, instead of the babies' long-suffering mother, their skittish father went with them to the NICU. The staff kept telling me I could touch them and kiss them. I wanted to, but I was terrified of hurting them or passing on some deadly cootie infection. They were so tiny, not much bigger than my hand. I'm a klutz when I'm screwing in a light bulb, so God only knows the damage I could do to a premature newborn the size of a burrito. The NICU staff just laughed and guided me to my children.

Hayley was four pounds. She had a light layer of strawberry blond hair and looked like she was smiling even when she wasn't, kind of like a Samoyed. She had some bruises on her face from being wrenched from beneath the siblings that had dog-piled her during the delivery. She was beautiful and the first to give a big, unmistakable grin. In one of the first pictures I took of her, she's smirking and winking at the camera, as if to say, "Wassup, yo?"

Ella was five pounds, three ounces. When I saw her, my jaw dropped. It was me as a baby—chunky with a full head of brown hair. We're talking a Chia-Pet mane at thirty-three weeks. Thankfully, Shelley's genetic contribution turned things around and made Ella beautiful in spite of looking like her dad. The nurse told me to lift up Ella's head and pose for a picture. When I did, her head rolled out of my hand and bonked into the side of the incubator. She let out a scream, and I freaked. She'd only been in the world twenty minutes and I'd given her brain damage. The nurse assured me that I hadn't hurt her.

"Don't worry," he said. "She'll hit her head much worse than that learning to walk." I think he meant it to make me feel better.

Emma was four pounds, one ounce, with a pixie dusting of brown hair. When I put my finger in her hand, she grabbed tight and wouldn't let go. I'll never forget the moment I saw her eyes: Caribbean blue with a perpetual twinkle. Even when she cried, the sparkle never left her eyes. She looked like a playful sprite out of an Irish fairy tale. She cried the least in those first days, though she changed that in a hurry when she got home.

Then there was Jordan, at four pounds, eight ounces. When I saw him, my heart dropped into my stomach. A respiratory therapist was fitting him with an oxygen tube. His lungs weren't fully developed, and he was having difficulty breathing. His tiny chest, no bigger than my palm, was going up and down in toil. His face was strained, a furrowed little brow over eyes closed tight. The alarm on his oxygen saturation monitor kept screaming as the numbers dropped.

Dr. Hinkes, the chief of the NICU, tried to explain to me what was going on, but I kept pressing him for a bottom line. Every answer he gave me began with, "Well ..." followed by a list of qualifiers. At last, he told me that this was a common condition for premature boys, and that there was a lot that they could do for him. Dr. Hinkes didn't seem worried, but that didn't keep me from worrying.

I spent hours in the NICU over the next few days. I sat next to the incubators and sang to my children. We weren't allowed to hold them yet, so I let them hold me. They clutched my finger as I gazed at them in loving wonder. Jordan wouldn't let go, holding on as he labored to breathe. His eyes would open a crack and he'd look at me, as if to say, "Dad ... I'm ... really ... tired. This ... sucks." My daughters, except for some manageable preemie woes, were healthy and growing. I praised God for that before begging him to help my son.

God's mood seemed to have changed since those maddening days during the pregnancy. The Jesus who had kept me in the dark and made me wait was now specializing in instant gratification. God had given me a U2 song titled "Miracle Drug" to keep me going through the pregnancy. Now he was about to supply the real thing.

Three days after the delivery, Jordan was having a rough time. A brawny, jocular respiratory therapist I liked was taking care of him. He flipped through Jordan's chart, looking irritated.

"Why don't we have him on Serfactin?" he said to one of the nurses. The nurse mumbled something back, and the respiratory therapist went to the phone. I don't know who he was talking to, but he sounded adamant. He put down the receiver and walked over to me.

"We're going to treat your son with a medication called Serfactin," he said. "We'll have to intubate him because it's sprayed into his lungs. He'll be uncomfortable for a little while, but I think it will really help."

"Does it usually work in cases like this?" I asked.

The respiratory therapist said — and I'm not making this up — "It's a miracle drug. I'm surprised it hasn't worked me out of a job."

A few days later, Jordan was off oxygen and breathing on his own. The first time I picked him up, he opened his eyes and looked at me. I started crying right in front of the nurse.

For months on my car stereo, Bono had been singing, "I'm not giving up on a miracle drug." God had been letting me know all along that things were going to be okay. My God isn't just Savior, Creator, Sustainer, and King; he's an artist. I'd been looking for billboards while he whispered to me in poetry.

God doesn't have to perform quick fixes or parlor tricks. He works on his own schedule. Sometimes God might let us rush him or change his mind, but it's generally not a good idea to try.

You don't pester a master chef while he's in the kitchen. God slow cooks his miracles using a lot of ingredients. He uses family, friends, science, and even music. But he asks us to add some ingredients too, like faith, hope, and love—especially love. The people around us supplied that in abundance. I wanted fast relief, but God had something much better in mind all along.

Shelley's pregnancy ended well, but not everyone's does. People filled with faith, hope, and love suffer unimaginable loss. Other babies in the NICU with our kids didn't survive. The few days of life they had were spent in pain. Some of those who did survive will be disabled for life. We went through a rough time, but a lot of the parents we met had it much harder. I know God loves them and has a plan, but it still breaks my heart. It's aggravating that such tragedy won't make sense until we get to heaven. I praise God for our miracle, but I still protest on behalf of those who lost the children they longed to love and hold.

Not that we got off easy. The miracle we'd received was about to smack us around like a heavyweight boxer in the ring with a jockey.

9

Good
Problems

THE CATHETER WAS TOO BIG FOR EMMA AND SHE WAS screaming. The more she screamed, the more frightened and angry I became. Why would they put a two-month-old, premature baby through so many useless tests? She was in the emergency room because she had stopped breathing for a few seconds and turned purple. By the time we had the 911 operator on the phone, she was breathing fine. It seemed like some spit had gone down the wrong way, temporarily choking her. They sent an ambulance anyway, just to make sure that she was okay.

The ambulance took us to a busy hospital nearby—not the one where the children were born, where everyone knew us. We had landed there on July Fourth weekend, so the ER was crowded. We were in a big room with other beds that were separated by dividers. A few feet away, a police officer interviewed a teenager with a gunshot wound, asking him which gang he was in. There was a lot of noise and chaos. In the midst of all this, Emma was screaming because some genius decided that her urinary tract needed to be checked—because that's the first thing you think of when someone stops breathing. The catheter was too big for a premature newborn, and Emma was in agony.

Tears drowned her beautiful blue eyes. She squeezed Shelley's fingers, howling as her face turned red. I could see in Shelley's face how angry she was that her daughter had to endure this. Finally, the nurse relented and Shelley scooped Emma up in her arms.

No more than two minutes later, a phlebotomist showed up. He said he needed to draw blood samples. I'd seen this done at the NICU. He was going to slice Emma's heel with a lancet until he got enough blood. With a preemie, it takes a long time to get enough blood.

"No," I told him. "She's just beginning to calm down. We need to give her a break."

"I need to do this now," he said.

"No way."

The poor guy could see in my eyes that the conversation was over. I wasn't about to submit my daughter to another round of torture. He might as well have asked me to pull daisies out of my nose.

Every test they gave Emma came back negative. She was fine. They wanted to hold her overnight anyway. They kept Emma in a big, cold antiseptic room with Plexiglass walls. She looked like an exhibit in the nocturnal marsupial house at the zoo. Shelley decided to sleep in the chair next to her and I went home to help Shelley's mom and my sister Lisa, who was visiting from Florida, take care of the other kids.

That night, pandemonium erupted on the floor of the hospital where Shelley and Emma were trying to sleep. A teenager died, and the family responded by going into a rage. They threatened hospital staff and ran down the hall cursing and screaming.

Since the walls to the room were clear, Shelley saw and heard all of this. She was terrified.

When I arrived at the hospital the next day, I was livid. My wife, already running on no more than a couple hours of sleep, caught only a few ten-minute snatches of slumber during that crazy night. We also had three other babies at home who needed our attention. Emma was fine, but they wanted to keep her another day. I told the charge nurse that I wanted to talk to the doctor. She said that he'd had a busy night and wasn't coming in until tomorrow. She told me that he'd see Emma then. She didn't know that she was talking to a clinical psychologist who'd done some of his training in a hospital.

"I guess I'll have to call Patient's Rights," I said.

"Excuse me?"

"By law, patients in a hospital must see their primary physician once every twenty-four hours. If the doctor isn't here by 7 o'clock this evening, I'm calling Patient's Rights."

I told you I'm a jerk ...

"I'll give him a call," the nurse said.

... but it pays off once in a while.

The doctor discharged Emma two hours later. She returned home to a festive welcome. For a little while, things were happy. Emma escaped the Chamber of Hospital Horrors because I'd been assertive. My personality had helped for a change, and I was proud.

I would not feel that way again for a very long time.

◦ ◦ ◦

We moved right after the kids were born. We left our beloved

172

townhouse in the idyllic foothill town of Sierra Madre for a house across the street from Shelley's parents. The move was crucial in many ways. Our new house was much better suited to raising babies than our multi-tiered townhouse with white carpets. Shelley's parents would be nearby to help. Even our dogs benefited because they had their own yard now. Our new home was a tremendous blessing that made life so much easier.

Notice I said *easier*. It was still the hardest time of my entire life.

The kids came home from the hospital one at a time, when each could drink formula instead of having it shoved through a tube in their nose. Soon after we'd moved all our stuff into the new house, the babies had all made it home. They were around six weeks old. I took a few weeks off from work to help with the kids and get us settled. But there was one small problem—we couldn't unpack. Caring for the children took every second and every last bit of energy we had, so we couldn't set up our new home. As a result, the kids, my wife, and I moved in with Shelley's parents.

Putting it nicely, my personality wasn't a good fit for our living situation. I'm ridiculously independent. I don't like anyone telling me what to do, messing with my schedule, or intruding on my space. I also hate details. The minutiae of life drive me insane. The more patience and concentration something requires, the more crazy it makes me. Now let me tell you about the first few weeks with our kids, and you can do the math on how well I handled it.

The kids had to be fed every three hours, 24/7. Vickie, Todd, Shelley, and I took shifts in twos. The babies were still getting used to drinking formula. We had to position the bottles and the babies' tiny heads just right or they wouldn't drink. We also had to keep them awake while they were eating, which was almost impossible. We frequently had to give a baby what we called a "water bomb" to keep him or her awake. This involved dabbing their head with a cold, wet washcloth. This was especially important because the babies were prone to having "A's and B's" (apneas and bradycardias) while they were eating. In other words, they would stop breathing and their heart rates would plummet. If *that* happened, we had to tickle the baby until they woke up. Sometimes this would take almost a minute, just long enough for me to go into cardiac arrest.

Good times.

But the real fun of A's and B's were the sleep monitors. Two babies had wires attached to their chests that measured heart rate and respiration. These wires ran to a machine that was a little bigger than a shoebox. When a kid had an A and B, the sleep monitor would wail like an air-raid siren, waking up everyone in the house and the people next door. It also made the same sound whenever its battery was low or a wire came loose. Remember, we had two of these.

After feeding came vitamin drops and medication. Using a dropper, we would squirt a precise amount into a nipple and try to get the baby to suck it in. The baby would often spit it up and we'd have to start over. The eye drops were even more fun than that. Try to keep a baby from blinking when you squirt liquid in her eye. We also had to keep the vitamin drops, eye drops, and medications for each child separated.

Before and after each feeding came the diaper changing. This was easier for me than I thought. When I'd seen other people change babies on airplanes or at picnics, I developed a mild urge to vomit. I soon discovered that it's very different with your own kids. The excrement was not a problem for me. The frailty of our children was another story. I had to move their heads and limbs with delicate precision, or they would flop around like dolls made of Jell-O. This made changing a diaper take awhile—and we did a lot of changing. People ask me how many diapers we went through—about 250 a week. Pampers stock must have skyrocketed. We dumped three large bags of diapers a day. We even had to order another dumpster from the city to contain our massive waste output. A hundred years from now, scientists will discover that our family alone tipped the scales on global warming.

The feedings, diaper changes, and medications all had to be recorded on a special chart. Since they were premature and still at risk, the doctors wanted us to keep track of how much each child was eating, when they got their medication, how often they went to the bathroom, and the precise nature of what showed up in the diaper when they did. For someone who hates details, this was nonstop fun.

After the feeding and the diapers and the charting came the cleaning. Since premature newborns are susceptible to infection, we had to sanitize everything, all the time. Bottles, nipples, the pitchers used to make formula, pacifiers, and anything that came into contact with the babies had to be washed by hand. The sink had to be scrubbed with vinegar and baking soda after each use to ensure that no microscopic urchins got ahold of our vulnerable children.

Next came making formula. The fun part about this was that each baby was on a different formula because they had different types of allergies and tolerances. Because Emma had food allergies, she was on the "Rolls Royce" formula that was so expensive it would have been cheaper to feed her Chateaubriand. We had to mix four different batches everyday, stirring endlessly so that clumps of powder wouldn't clog up the bottle.

This entire process took almost three hours. Then, ninety minutes later, it began again. We hadn't organized our volunteers very well, so Shelley, her parents, and I handled most of this during the first few weeks.

My life became a blur of infinitesimal details upon details. I had to manage a dozen different things with precision and care, and all of them were tiny and fragile. I had to focus, concentrate, and remember like I never had in my life. I forgot things and made mistakes. I'd measure the formula wrong, miss stuff while cleaning, or forget to write important details on the chart. I was slow and inept at every important task. And I had to do everything through the fog of sleep deprivation. My few sleep breaks were restless, even though I was exhausted. I tossed in bed anxiously awaiting the next sound of a crying baby. I got in the habit of keeping a can of Red Bull on my nightstand. When a baby (or two or three or four) sounded off long enough that I knew it wasn't a false alarm, I rolled out of bed, downed the caffeinated elixir in three gulps, and staggered off to duty.

I might have been able to keep my sanity if I was in my own home, with my own bed and my own stuff, but I was living with Shelley's parents. Every single comfort and diversion was packed up across the street. I had no privacy or freedom. My waking hours were filled with excruciating attention to detail. Everything that I enjoyed and did well was gone. Replacing it was everything that I hated and did terribly. The end was nowhere in sight because we couldn't unpack and set up our new home, even though it was less than a hundred feet away. The rare times we weren't working, we had three options: sleep, shower, or unpack. During the first two weeks after the kids were home, I chose to go unpack only once. I made it for less than thirty minutes before passing out on a bare mattress.

The only moments of grace I experienced during the first month were the times I held my children in my arms and stared into their eyes. The good news is that I did this a lot. Though they were the cause of this hurricane, they were also its eye. When they cooed, coughed, and cuddled in my arms, it no longer felt like I was sentenced to prison and hard labor. The thing that still spins my head around is that some of the best moments of my life came during the worst time of my life. Falling asleep on the couch with one of my tiny children tucked into my chest made me feel quiet and full—and quiet and full are tall orders for me. I can remember those times fondly now. At the time, however, they were fleeting moments of relief, glimpses of sunshine through a crack in the prison wall.

The worst point came one morning when I had three precious hours to sleep. Within a few seconds of slipping beneath the cool sheet, I was comatose. I floated beneath the sort of deep, paralyzed, open-mouthed, drooling sleep where you don't even dream. Not a log in the world could've competed with me. In the middle of this unconscious bliss, Shelley walked into the room and woke me up. Dick and Margie, a saintly couple from St. Luke's, had arrived with a beautiful crib that had belonged to their grandchild. Shelley needed me to get up and help unload it.

There's a particular type of rage that shows up only when someone is roused from deep slumber. It's primitive. The parts of the brain that inhibit animalistic behavior are still asleep. I don't remember exactly what I said to Shelley, but I remember how it sounded. I emitted something guttural and monstrous. I was like a hibernating bear roaring at an intruder. Shelley shouted something back at me and stormed out of the room. A couple of minutes later, the rest of my brain yawned, stretched, blinked, and told me, "They can't unload that crib without you, jerk. Stop being so selfish and go help."

I downed my reserve can of Red Bull and tossed myself out of bed. My mother-in-law was standing in the living room.

"Where's Shelley?" I asked.

"She went to help with the crib," she said, deadpan. "She was crying."

I didn't say anything and stormed out the front door. As I staggered across the street, I felt something terrible and over-whelming. The intensity of it halted me in the middle of the street.

I'm in hell, I thought. *I'm not allowed to sleep, and my life is filled with mind-numbing tasks that I'm terrible at. I have no home of my own. The private conflicts of my marriage are laid bare for my mother-in-law to witness. I'm trapped, and there's nothing I can do. There is no peace, no rest, and certainly no fun. God, you have to do something.*

I don't hear God talk very often, and when I do, I never know if it's him or my unconscious mind belching up what I want to hear. But this time, I'm pretty sure God was talking.

Why don't you *do something?* he said. *The only reason it feels like you're in prison is that you haven't bothered to look for the keys. You're not the prisoner — you just think everyone else is your warden — Shelley, Vickie, even the babies. Maybe you need to stop acting like a victim and do something about this.*

Existentialists say that a man does not know who he is until he looks into the abyss. When he reaches the point where he loses hope, he has only two choices: despair or responsibility. Standing in the middle of that street in my wrinkled, stinky clothes, I looked into the abyss. I considered despair for a long time. I thought about ways I could give up and escape. Only after I cried out to God did I see responsibility as an option. Even though I had children, I wasn't a father yet. I had not made this burden my own. I behaved like it was somebody else's burden that I'd been forced to carry at gunpoint. When I asked God for help, he did not rescue me.

He told me I had a job to do.

A couple of nights later, between feedings, three babies started crying at once. Actually, howling is more like it. It was my shift, but usually someone woke up and helped when they heard this kind of commotion. So I waited, listening for footsteps. Nothing. My first response was aggravation. Why wasn't anybody getting up to help? Then, the one molecule of altruism left in my brain sputtered to life. Maybe I could handle this and give my exhausted wife and mother-in-law a break. I tried singing and cooing to the babies, but they kept screaming until my ears rang. I had no choice but to rock them back to sleep.

I put one baby over a shoulder and scooped the other two into my forearms. I eased into a rocking chair, terrified that I'd drop one and disable them for life. When I made it to a sitting position, I nestled a baby in each arm. Then I crossed my legs and cradled the third in the crook of my knee. I started rocking. In a few minutes, everybody was asleep. I felt proud of myself until I realized that I'd overlooked a minor problem—I couldn't get up. Any attempt would wake them.

The feeling of being in prison returned, but I decided to dam the flood of self-pity for a change. I looked at the children adorning my body. Soft, tiny pillows of warmth covered me. They were beautiful. More than that, they were alive. And I was caring for them by myself. I felt like a competent father for the first time. I'd had nice paternal moments with them individually, but this was the first time I felt like a man caring for his children. I smiled as my fatigue and aggravation dissipated. I was glad that no one else had gotten out of bed. If they had, I wouldn't have forced myself to rock three at once. I wouldn't have had this moment of grace and quiet with my kids. When Shelley came in the room awhile later, she consecrated the moment with five words.

"Wow. Look at you, Superdad."

I smiled at her. We shared our first nice moment in a long time. Then I said, "I have to go to the bathroom," and she helped me put the kids in their cribs.

Though rocking three of my children at once was incredible, it made something clear to me: we needed help. Lots of it. If it takes a village to raise a child, we were going to need a metropolis.

I sent an email to every person that we knew in Southern California. I told them that we needed help. This is not something I like to do. I don't like people helping me with things, because it makes me feel obligated. I have a very hard time believing that people will help and expect nothing in return. I have an even harder time believing that they will *enjoy* it. I was about to be proven wrong.

Two days later, reinforcements arrived. Friends, family members, and church members by the dozen flooded into Todd and Vickie's home. They took over feeding shifts, washed bottles, made formula, and rocked babies to sleep. I started gaining weight as someone showed up every day with a steaming casserole of cheese and carbohydrates. Margie, the woman from our church who'd brought the crib, offered to organize our volunteers. She was like General Patton—only nicer and prettier—commanding the tank divisions that broke through the German lines to relieve the beleaguered and starving 101st Airborne in the Battle of the Bulge. She screened volunteers and organized them into an efficient and effective schedule.

My family also flew in from Kentucky to help. My sisters, Suzanne and Lisa, each came out for a week to help. Even my brother-in-law Tom threw his hat in the ring. My high school buddy Kevin used frequent flyer miles and vacation time so he could come pitch in. My parents flew out and worked like beavers even though they were in their mid-seventies. Things were hard for them because they were on the other side of the continent. They couldn't participate in their grandchildren's lives like our friends and Shelley's family could. It was a sad irony that they longed to be part of this circus while the rest of us longed for a break.

A cloud of accomplices surrounded us, giving us rest. We even got six hours of sleep sometimes. And we were finally able to move into our house. We had lots of help with that too. Shelley's parents and their friends slaved endlessly to help set up our new home. Of course, they probably wanted the daycare center out of their living room, but they still blessed us beyond measure. We were getting closer to a normal everyday life. Well, as normal as life with newborn quadruplets can be.

But things were still hard. Shelley and her mother were overworked and exhausted. I was like an employee working shifts, but they were the managers who oversaw the whole operation. Breaks were scarce, even for eating. When Shelley and I went out for dinner on her birthday, we realized that we were inhaling our food because we were so used to eating on the fly. The volunteers helped us survive, but the babies were the only ones thriving. Shelley's body was wracked with pain. The pregnancy had overwhelmed and eroded her body, and she had had no time to recover. She suffered painful arthritis in her joints until the kids were a year old. Time became fluid, with day and night becoming peripheral events in a nonstop schedule. My extremities started to tingle, and the doctor told me it was from poor circulation due to lack of sleep. Everyone was cranky—though, if we were having a contest, I would have won.

Even with the help of volunteers, I knew we couldn't be the kind of parents—much less husband and wife—that we wanted to be unless we got some rest. Despair started to creep back in, but help was on the way. God was about to send us an angel.

An overnight nanny was the only thing that would keep us from killing ourselves or each other. We had just enough money put away to hire somebody for a year. The problem was finding that somebody. We didn't want a complete stranger caring for our fragile children, so we sought strong referrals. We got a few and contacted them, but nobody returned our calls. Apparently, the childcare professionals of Southern California weren't eager for a graveyard shift with quadruplet newborns.

I was lamenting this problem one day when Kendra, one of

my students, had come over to help with the kids. She and her husband Ross were two of my best students. I'd worked with them since they started the PhD program five years before, and they had become friends more than students. She told me that Ross's sister Lauren was moving to Los Angeles and needed a job. Then he told me that her previous job had been caring for at-risk infants born to drug-addicted moms. Lauren was moving to L.A. to be near her boyfriend, Joey. Joey just happened to work for me in my private practice, another star student who had become a friend. In terms of connections, this young lady couldn't have done any better.

I got Lauren's phone number and gave her a call. I liked her almost immediately. She sounded kind, intelligent, and excited about working for us. I also detected a dry sense of humor and a hint of sarcasm. There's no faster way to score points with me, but I decided to interrogate her a little anyway.

"How many kids at a time did you take care of at your previous job?"

"Four."

"No way," I said, laughing. "You're just making that up."

"I'd be glad to give you my supervisor's number if you'd like to confirm it with her."

I didn't even need to see her résumé after that. After Shelley talked to her for a few minutes, we were sold.

Lauren started working for us the same day we moved into our new house. At first, Shelley and I took turns helping her during the night. In a few days, however, she reassured us that she could handle things by herself. She was right. Occasionally, three or four would go ballistic at the same time and she'd need our help. Otherwise, Shelley and I returned to almost normal sleep habits. Life was still insane, but we were in our own home sleeping at least a few hours a night in our own beds.

God had scaled back on the divine intervention stuff ever since the kids left the hospital. It was probably a good thing. We needed to hunker down and adjust to our new life instead of skipping from miracle to miracle. Instead of letting us walk on water, God threw us into the deep end of the pool so we'd learn how to swim. But when Lauren came to work for us, we saw God's hand again. She needed a job. We needed a nanny that we could trust. God lined us up like puzzle pieces.

With all the help from friends and family and Lauren handling things at night, we finally got some rest. We didn't feel on the verge of death all the time, and Shelley's body began to heal.

Still, everything was different. I had lost the privacy, freedom, and control that I'd cherished ever since I was hiding out in my basement cave as a teenager. You see, I've run from living in community my whole life. I love socializing, but that's different. You can leave a party anytime you want. Life in community is ordinary and constant. I looked forward to getting out of Shelley's parents' house and into our home because I thought things would be more like my old life. I didn't understand that I was part of a community now. I didn't live in a cave anymore; I lived in a village. No, a metropolis. In my living room!

Over time, family life got easier. I didn't get frustrated or bored as easily. I became better at cleaning things and paying attention to detail. Shelley didn't have to remind me to do things as often. I griped less and worked harder. But it's not like I was happy about it. I learned to survive in the matriarchal nest, but I still didn't understand my place. I white-knuckled my way through this new life without embracing it. I was desperate for motion, stimulation, and freedom. I still didn't understand why God had picked me for this assignment.

• • •

My six-week "vacation" from work ended when the kids were about ten weeks old. When I got into my car to go back to work, it felt like a prison break. For a few hours, I could sit alone in my office and take back the reins of my life. As Clinical Director of Fuller's counseling center, I had authority and control. Only two or three people could tell me what to do, and they usually left me alone. For a little while, I was free again. I cruised down the freeway, blasting my stereo, and smiling. I'd never been so happy to go to work ... until I walked into the office.

Pictures of my kids were everywhere. I'd loaded over a hundred photos on a web site, and our office manager Beth had printed out every one. They were plastered all over the bulletin board and the front desk. It paralyzed me. I stood and gazed in wonder at Hayley, Ella, Jordan, and Emma. They were beautiful. I was in love with them. When I woke up that morning, I wanted nothing more than to get to the office. Once I was there, all I wanted to do was go home.

The contradiction was too much for me. I walked into my office, shut the door, and fell asleep on my desk.

10

Wonder Woman

HERE'S A TYPICAL SCENE FROM THE FIRST YEAR WITH the kids: I'm in the kitchen making Emma's formula. Powders, measuring cups, pitchers, strainers, and scales are everywhere. It looks like a crystal meth lab. The kitchen is messier than usual because I'm the one making the formula. When I'm almost done, Shelley comes in and sees me pouring the formula into bottles.

"Are there any chunks in the formula?" Shelley asks.

"I dunno," I say. "No, I don't think so."

"Well, did you strain it?"

"Strain it? Why would I have to strain it? I used the electric mixer so it should be fine."

"Did you clean the beaters before you used the mixer?"

"I rinsed them off."

Shelley sighs and says, "You have to wash them with soap. Jordan's formula has soy in it, and Emma is allergic to soy. If any of his powder gets into Emma's mix, she'll get sick."

I look at Shelley like she just cussed at me in a foreign language.

"You have to start over again," she says.

"What?! I've been working for like an hour! No way. It'll be fine."

"Then I'll have to do it, I guess. I don't want Emma getting sick."

"Unbelievable! Fine, I'll do it."

"And don't forget to strain it," Shelley says. "The chunks clog up the nipples, and the kids won't finish their bottles."

I clench my teeth, throw the plastic pitcher into the sink, and start to wash it in a way that suggests I'm trying to smash it.

This kind of thing happened every day. Shelley became frustrated with me because I'd forget things and miss a lot of details. Even when I was trying hard, I had to ask for specific directions, making more work for my exhausted wife. I got aggravated because I didn't know my place. If caring for the children involved so many things that I didn't do well, what did I bring to the family? I got tired of feeling like the only one who didn't know what was going on. I became irritable and contentious with my wife because I resented the fact that she was so good at so many things I wasn't.

Our friends and church volunteers thought Shelley was a superhero. They heaped adulation upon her, and she deserved every bit of it. The only problem was that they sometimes praised her by contrasting her with me.

One morning I was one my way out the door to work. The house was a blur of activity with Shelley at the center. The scene was stressful and intense, but she managed to cover everything from screaming babies to dirty diapers to preparing formula. I entered the living room showered, shaved, and wearing work clothes, about to head out the door and leave behind my harried wife who hadn't showered all week.

One of the volunteers from church saw me and said, "It must be nice to go to work."

I smiled and nodded in agreement, though I felt like saying, "How would you like to try running a large outpatient mental health facility on four hours of sleep?"

But the volunteer wasn't finished.

"I read in *USA Today* that raising children is twice as hard as a full-time job. I guess Shelley is working enough for both of you."

"You've got that right!" I said, though in my head I said, "*What did* USA Today *say is the hourly equivalent of calming down panicked first-year students with suicidal clients, de-escalating a psychotic patient throwing a fit in the waiting room, seeing four clients after 5:00 p.m., and then coming home and feeding babies in the middle of the night?*"

I left for work in a foul mood, feeling guilty for leaving and angry that everyone seemed to think I was a slacker.

That night, I got home late after seeing clients. A chorus of "Shhhh!" greeted me when I walked through the door. Shelley, her mom, and her dad were trying to rock babies to sleep and they weren't about to let me wake them up and create another hour of work. I felt like an intruder in my own home.

The following night I got home later than usual because I was stuck in traffic. It had been a horrible commute, all the more because I was desperate to spend time with the kids before they were in bed. I started shouting at the immobile traffic from inside my car.

"What's the matter with you people? There's no accident, no police chase. Nobody's shooting a movie on the side of the freeway today. Why don't you all just *move*? Don't you know that I'm dying to see my kids and you're all keeping me from them?"

When I finally pulled into the driveway, I flung the door open and jumped out of the car. I raced toward the front door, hoping I wasn't too late to kiss my children good night. When I was almost there, the door opened and one of the volunteers came out of the house.

"The kids are asleep," she said, "but it took awhile to get them down. It's been a rough night. I guess *you* picked a good time to get home."

The woman who said this is an angel, and I'm sure she was just trying to be funny. Or maybe she really was frustrated that I hadn't arrived in time to help. That would be easy to understand. Nevertheless, her words sent me over the edge. But she wasn't finished.

"Shelley has it tough," she said. "I hope you're finding ways to give her a break."

This time, I didn't have enough patience to toss her a polite response.

"Let's see ... I'm working my butt off at two jobs trying to make enough money to support a family of six and then working on a book after everyone goes to sleep. I'm also trying to save money for a house and college tuition. Do you have any other suggestions?"

The poor lady's face turned red and she said, "I was just kidding. I know you're working as hard as you can."

I went from feeling indignant to feeling like a jerk.

"I'm sorry," I said. "It's just been a bad day."

She gave me a hug that I didn't deserve and told me to go inside and relax.

I was embarrassed that I'd lost my cool with a woman who'd been so kind and giving. Still, what did everyone think? That I was trying to shuck responsibility? That I gallivanted off to my job every day as a way to get out of the "real" work? Did anybody think that I played any significant role in our family? Was I nothing more than a drone bringing honey back to the hive while the Queen Bee did the important stuff?

I didn't know who I was anymore. All the things that I thought made me who I was—being clever, funny, and being a leader—meant nothing in the New Quadruplet Order. Where Shelley is detail-oriented, I'm more of a "big picture" person. If I were captain of a ship, for example, I would be great at charting the best course toward a destination. If we ran into a storm, you'd want me at the helm. However, I wouldn't want to be bothered with the specifics of hoisting the sails. Shelley, on the other hand, would know the best way to position the sails, how to tie all the knots, and the last time the sails went to the cleaners. Our new life was all about focus and details. Shelley was doing the work that mattered. Our children needed a woman like her.

One Friday night after work, I brought Shelley some flowers to show my appreciation. I even had a nice speech ready.

"Honey," I said, bouquet in hand, "our children are growing and flourishing because of you. I couldn't do what you do in a million years. Even though you're a talented psychologist, you prefer being home with our children, and that blesses all of us."

"Thanks," Shelley said. "But if you really want to show how much you appreciate me, you can start leaving yourself notes around the house so you don't forget things as often."

I could have responded to that with humility. I could have admitted the fact that—surprise, surprise—I wasn't good at everything. I could have submitted to my wife's guidance when it came to caring for our children. But submission is not something I do very well. Getting defensive, however, is.

"I don't believe this," I said. "I try to do something nice and you remind me what a screw-up I am. I feel like I'm getting edged out of my family. You don't respect me or appreciate my contributions."

"Hon," she said, "I totally appreciate everything you do, and I'm sorry if I don't say so more. But I feel like I'm in over my head and your impatience makes it worse. It would be difficult for any wife to tolerate a negative attitude from her husband under normal circumstances. Throw newborn quadruplets into the mix and it becomes impossible. *I'm* the one in the middle of all this chaos. I'm taking care of the kids. I'm managing everything related to them. I organize the volunteers, shopping lists as long as your arm, household chores, doctor's appointments, prescriptions, insurance claims, and I spend my down time researching the best way to care for premature infants. I never get a good night's sleep, and it's nonstop stress when I'm awake ..."

"All right, already!" I shouted. "I can't win a contest about who works harder. I'll try to do more, but I feel like I'm losing my mind!" I stomped out to my makeshift office in the garage to eat my dinner alone.

Though our children provided endless moments of joy, neither of us had time to relax. Shelley never stopped working. By the time the kids were six months old, my wife hadn't just reached her physical and mental limits, she'd been pushed beyond them.

I was at the end of my rope too. I made it a point to relax by watching television at night, but I did it at the expense of sleep. I usually got around four hours a night. Two stubborn people plus four newborns minus four hours of sleep equals marriage meltdown.

When the kids were six months old, we went crazy. I don't mean that as euphemism. We did not develop a full-blown psychotic disorder like Schizophrenia, but we had bona fide psychotic symptoms. The most common of these was paranoid delusion.

"What are you doing at work today?" Shelley asked one morning as I went out the door.

"Don't accuse me of slacking off!" I said. "I work just as hard as you do!"

"What are you talking about? Why are you snapping at me?"

"Don't talk to me that way!" I said and went out the door.

Two days later, Shelley and I were in the bedroom during a rare quiet moment. Shelley was staring at her computer screen.

"Are you looking at porn again?" I joked, but she didn't laugh.

"I'm looking at our online banking statement. I need to have access to all of our money."

"You do," I said. "I sent you an email that told you how to access the accounts online."

"So? How do I know that you're not hiding some money somewhere?

"What? Why would I do that?"

"Maybe you plan to run away."

"Have you lost your marbles?"

"Don't talk to me that way!" Shelley shouted and went to check on the kids.

By the time the kids were seven months old, almost every conversation we had was like this. I started spending more time in my office out back so I wouldn't have to talk to Shelley. Then, one day in November, she came back to my office. She slid back the sliding glass door and just stood there, staring at me as I typed on the computer.

"What?" I demanded.

"Why are you always back here whenever the kids are asleep?"

"You know why. I'm not as likely to have a brain hemorrhage from you yelling at me."

"You yell more than I do." She was right about this, but I didn't care.

"Will you please leave me alone? Why do you want to start a fight?"

"Because I'm terrified of us getting a divorce."

"It seems like you'd be the one to do that. Seems like you think I'm just a burden. I feel like you would divorce me in a second."

"Never say that. It would never happen. Tell me it will never happen."

I glowered at her. I wanted to tell her that it could. I wanted to say that I was miserable and that I felt like she didn't need me anymore. I felt like throwing in the towel. But I couldn't. I would never let it get to that. I didn't like Shelley at the moment, but I still loved her. And God had given us a tremendous blessing and huge responsibility. As crazy as I was, I wasn't ready to give up.

"We need help," I said. "I don't care how much it costs. We have to get marriage counseling."

Tears started running down Shelley's face. "Okay," she said. "You set it up and I'll go."

I started asking around for a good marital therapist. Since Shelley and I are psychologists, we had good connections that led us to a great marital therapist. When the kids were a little over seven months old, we started seeing Dr. Phil Ringstrom (no, not *that* Dr. Phil). Even though I'm a shrink, I was a bit wary of marital therapy. A lot of it seems to skirt around core issues, wasting time on things like communication skills and "I" statements. But Phil changed my mind.

We made an appointment and went to his office. He worked out of a house instead of a regular office building. The waiting room was the living room. Shelley and I sat on the couch, chatting nervously. We'd been on the other end of this exchange, but had no idea what it was like to be the counselees and not the counselor in couples therapy.

A door opened and there stood ... a rock star. Phil had long blond hair and a neatly trimmed beard. He was wearing black jeans and a matching black shirt. He looked like my college saxophone teacher who played in a blues band. Not what I was expecting.

Phil smiled broadly and invited us in. We all sat down and Phil looked at us and smiled, but said nothing. That might have freaked us if it wasn't a technique we'd both used before. I told Shelley she could start.

She told him about the quadruplets and his jaw dropped.

"Wow. I'm not surprised this has affected your marriage."

Shelley continued, telling Phil how aggravated she was with

me. When my turn came, I told him how Shelley made me insane. Phil nodded and listened for about twenty minutes, then he spoke.

"You guys are taking your stress out on each other because there's nowhere else to take it. Having quadruplets has overwhelmed you completely, but you can't get mad at anyone but each other. You certainly aren't going to take it out on the kids—you seem like good parents and it sounds like you seldom express so much as annoyance toward the babies. Shelley, you're not going to start snapping at the volunteers from church. Steve, you can't yell at your clients or students. This means that, at the end of the day, your marriage consists of two punching bags. The problem is that both of you feel like a punching bag without realizing that you're also throwing punches."

Over the next few weeks, Phil helped us understand what happened when we fought. When people become enraged during an argument, they're no longer fighting about specific issues. Instead, they're trying to regain power. When a couple is fighting, each can feel like the victim and see the other as the abuser. Both experience the other one as dominating. Since nobody likes being dominated, they do and say things to regain a sense of control. If one person says something mean, the other feels compelled to say something meaner, even if it's not even in the neighborhood of reality or logic. This is called "auto-correction." It's a psychotic spiral that results in two people saying terrible things they don't mean just because they hate feeling victimized. Phil told us that the only thing to do in such a situation is to get away from each other for at least thirty minutes. It takes that long for the adrenaline-fueled "fight or flight" response to recede.

Phil also taught us what I came to think of as the Five Percent

Rule. In reality, less than five percent of the things Shelley did made me angry and vice versa. Though we were both happy with ninety-five percent of what the other did, we focused only on the five percent we didn't like. This put things in perspective. It helped us to talk about the ways that we appreciated each other instead of just focusing on the things that drove us nuts. Once we stopped expecting each other to be perfect, we realized how many good things thrived in our marriage.

This was all good and helpful stuff, but one day, Phil nailed me.

Shelley was complaining about how I always forget to lock the back door, and I couldn't keep quiet. I was reacting to every other word, sighing loudly or exclaiming something like, "That is not fair!" All of a sudden, Phil looked at me and said, "Wow. You are really sensitive."

"What?!" I said, ready to turn on him instead of Shelley.

"You get injured when someone sees your flaws. It sounds like you hate it when someone sees a weakness. You're okay if you can confess them on your own—that gives you control and makes you sound like some humble, emergent church guru."

Despite my anger, I started laughing.

"You know what I mean, don't you?"

"Um, yeah, I have to admit I do," I said and then Shelley started to laugh. Not at me, but with me.

"Whenever Shelley talks about something you do that she doesn't like, you react like she's just walked in on you while you're in the bathroom. 'Hey!' you shout. 'Get outta here! Close the door! You have no business in here. Give me some privacy!' It comes out as anger, but I think it really makes you feel ashamed."

Shelley threw an arm around me.

"Is that true, hon?" she asked. "I thought you were just angry and indignant, but is it true that you just don't like me seeing your flaws?"

I nodded my head and said nothing. Shelley gave me a hug. I felt vulnerable and exposed, but I also felt good. Phil had been able to say what I couldn't, and I was glad.

In that moment, things started to change. We started giving each other more grace. I started trying harder, and it worked because I was motivated by love for Shelley rather than fear and resentment. I stopped expecting Shelley to live with me and never utter a peep about the things she doesn't like. That would be hard enough without quadruplets. There was too much to do and too much at stake for Shelley to tiptoe around my hypersensitivity. Shelley and I started to see each other as we really were: broken, imperfect people who were trying to love each other and our kids.

Pop culture sells us a lie about romantic love. Books, movies, music, and television tell us that human love can be perfect. They lead us to believe that we will never feel disappointed. We long for a fantasy partner that will never hurt us and never make us nuts. We see movies like *Jerry Maguire* and start believing that another person can "complete" us. Only God can do that. Only God's love is perfect. Once I realized this, I stopped expecting Shelley to be perfect. See, I *am* sensitive. I want someone to convince me that I'm okay as I am. I want to believe that this forgetful, messy, impulsive guy is worth something. My wife can't convince me of that, even though she tries. My kids, as beautiful and loving as they are, can't do it either. My wife and kids can make me feel loved, but God is the only one who can complete me.

Once I realized this, I wasn't so psychotic anymore. I started seeing my wife for who she really is: a brilliant, diligent, funny, delightful woman with a heart overflowing with love. And sooooo beautiful. One of the best parts of getting over my anger and resentment was enjoying again just how darn sexy my wife is. That didn't hurt with the, um, reconciliation.

By forcing me to face up to my flaws, God taught me the same thing that he's been whacking me in the head with for years: I need to depend on him. The love I receive from my family and friends is crucial. It's one of the best ways God loves me, but I cannot expect other people to love me the way that God does. If I can remember that, maybe I won't be so stinking selfish all the time. Maybe I'll look to God for my sense of identity and self-esteem instead of demanding it from others. Maybe I won't expect strokes and praise even when I'm not good at something. Maybe I'll get over myself and start showing other people the kind of love that God shows me.

Through the stress of caring for newborns and the resulting conflicts with my wife, God showed me that my cynicism masked sensitivity. A smirking, frowning aloofness hid my fear that people would discover that I'm a flawed, cumbersome man. Living with four fragile babies exposed my flaws, mostly to my wife. She had to point them out if she was going to survive. Once I stopped defending myself and denying my deficiencies, God taught me that Shelley wasn't the only one who had to learn to live with them—I did too. I had to accept my imperfections and ask for grace. Once I did that, I found that my wife was not some matriarchal superstar with whom I could never compete.

As long as I'm honest with her about my weaknesses, she's my greatest ally. And whenever I bring my brokenness before God, he draws close and lets me know that it's okay. Being weak is part of the deal when we follow Christ. Cynicism doesn't allow much room for that. It covers up the broken heart that we're afraid to let anyone heal.

11

Thirteen
Hours

"DO YOU WANT TO SLEEP FIRST OR SECOND?" SHELLEY asked me.

It was the Friday after New Year's and we had just gotten the babies off to sleep. This was no small accomplishment. A mouse belch could wake up one of the kids, especially Ella, who inherited her father's nocturnal proclivity. She would start crying, and it would wake up Jordan. Jordan would wake up Emma. Hayley was a deep sleeper, but if the other three were howling, she'd join in the fun. Thus, getting the babies to sleep was like playing Jenga—make one wrong move and all your hard work crashes in futility.

Shelley and I were both exhausted, but there was no point in both of us going to bed. Every hour or so, there was something to be done for the kids. Even when the kids slept, we remained on edge, drifting in and out of consciousness in anticipation of the next baby alarm. Lauren worked the graveyard shift Sunday night through Friday morning. The weekends, however, were up to us. Shelley and I resorted to taking four-hour shifts. We looked forward to Sunday night like other people look forward to Friday night.

"I'll take both shifts tonight," I told Shelley.

She looked at me blankly. "You'll stay up all night?"

I nodded. "But then I'll have to sleep tomorrow."

She nodded, still looking a little unsure.

"Why don't we do this every weekend?" I offered. "I'll take the night shift and you take the day shift. We'll have them together in the evenings."

"You would do that?"

"I'd love to do that!" I felt silly for not figuring it out sooner. This would make it easier for Shelley to get a full night's sleep, and I wouldn't mind having the time to myself anyway.

When Shelley planted a big fat kiss on my lips, I knew I had done something right.

• • •

"No!" I shouted.

I couldn't believe what I was seeing. Everything had led up to this moment, and it changed everything. I had never expected something like this to happen.

Sharon just shot Commander Adama.

I was watching the season finale of *Battlestar Galactica*. Every week, I counted the hours until I could sit down sometime after midnight on a Friday with a plate of hot flautas from Costco and watch my favorite television show. I had to watch it on TiVo, of course, because I'd undoubtedly have to pause the show before I got to the end of it—one of the babies would need me. Sometimes I would pause the show and go do something else just to make it last longer. I hated seeing the credits roll because it started the clock on another week of waiting.

Another week before I got to see Starbuck get in and out of trouble. Another week before getting more clues about what the Cylons were up to. Seven whole days until my finest retreat from the world. Since this was the season finale, it would be months before I could watch *Battlestar* again.

I had finally found my place in the quadruplet factory. I discovered something I could do that no one else could: stay up all night and sleep all day. Even Lauren hated flipping her days and nights, and she pulled graveyard shift five nights a week. Before the kids were born, Shelley and I lamented the fact that our circadian rhythms didn't match. She's a morning person who likes to hop in bed around nine o'clock. Left to my own devices, I'll stay up until four and sleep until noon. At first, we considered this poor planning on God's part. After the kids were born, we saw that God knew what he was doing.

The credits rolled, and I stood up, stretching. Everyone was asleep, and I had my castle to myself. And this kingdom would be mine every Friday and Saturday night for a long time.

We usually got the last baby to sleep by ten o'clock. Once everyone was asleep, however, the house was mine. I loved our new weekend schedule so much that it felt like I was getting away with something. I took to the night shift like Bela Lugosi. Between the time the babies went down and the midnight feeding, I did chores. I washed dishes, emptied trash, made formula, swept the floors, and replaced dead batteries in the swinging, humming, lullabying contraptions that filled our home. Then I would get a jump on the midnight feeding by waking up one of the babies. I wasn't about to wait for *them* to wake up crying and start a domino effect that forced me to feed all four at once.

It could be done, but it was never pretty and I'd have to wake up Shelley for help.

The midnight feeding was the highlight of my night. The best moments with my children during their first year occurred at midnight on the weekends. If everything went smoothly, I got some rare time alone with each of my children. I'd gaze in their eyes while they ate. I'd whisper things like, "I'm your daddy and you're my daughter/son and I love you." I'd make silly noises that no adult was permitted to hear. When they were done feeding, I'd rock them and sing them to sleep. If I were ahead of schedule, I'd rock each one for a little while after they dozed off. When one of my children curled up in the crook of my arm and fell asleep, I felt quiet inside. Love became tangible, resting in my arms.

Though I made sure everybody got some cuddle time, nobody blamed me if I gave a little extra to Hayley. During the first year, Hayley was the easiest, so much so that we worried. She fussed the least, slept the most, and was the last to cause trouble. She was an angel. The only problem was that she sometimes got shortchanged on attention because she was so easygoing. So after Ella, Jordan, and Emma finished their midnight feedings, I made it a point to let Hayley sleep on my chest for a while. Sometimes I'd doze off with her. I didn't want her to miss out just because she wasn't a troublemaker.

After the midnight feeding came Steve time. I surfed the Internet, played video games, and wrote emails to friends. Most of all, however, I watched movies. I'd been in cinematic withdrawal ever since the kids were born. I'd watch one or two movies a night. In the wee hours of Saturday and Sunday mornings, I reclaimed my pre-quadruplet life for a few hours.

When dawn arrived, Shelley and I would see each other briefly. Our weekend relationship reminded me of a Matthew Broderick film from the 1980's called *Ladyhawke*. The movie is about two lovers under the spell of a jealous wizard. He casts a spell that causes the man to be a wolf during the night and the woman a hawk during the day. They could only see each other in human form at twilight. They would reach out for each other, almost touch, and then one of them would turn into a beast and go kill a squirrel or something. That was Shelley and me, only without the squirrel part.

"Good morning, honey," I'd say as she came into the living room while I was giving the kids breakfast.

"How did things go last night?" she'd ask, and then I'd give her a report, including the impressive amount of laundry and cleaning I'd done.

"Great work," she'd say with a hug.

Well, that's the way it happened sometimes. Other times, we'd snap at each other because I was ready to go to bed but she needed me to do something first. Still, it was nothing like our fights just a few months before.

Though I loved my nocturnal life on the weekends, it had drawbacks. We couldn't go to church anymore. Our kids were still too susceptible to infection to leave them in the nursery, and going to church would mean a full day without sleep for at least one of us. We'd become very involved in St. Luke's before the kids, so we felt the loss. On top of that, Mondays were always a rude awakening. On Sundays, I'd get out of bed around four in the afternoon, making it hard to fall asleep that night. Sometimes I would drink wine to bring on drowsiness, but the alcohol hurt the quality of my sleep. I slogged into work on

Monday mornings, mainlining Red Bull and scowling at anyone brave enough to speak to me. Though I enjoyed the time with my children and myself over the weekends, the erratic sleep schedule started to take its toll.

Not just on me, of course. At least twice a week, all four kids would awake at once and gang up on whoever had the night shift. This meant Shelley had to get out of bed in the middle of the night to help. When the children were awake, they demanded constant attention. When they were asleep, we never got any real rest because the kids didn't sleep through the night. Even when Lauren was working, it wasn't unusual for her to get waylaid by three or more. One of us would get up to help her, if for no other reason than we couldn't sleep through all the crying.

"The babies are going to be a year old soon," Shelley said one night after we had managed to get them all to sleep.

"Yeah. We'll have to throw a big bash."

"Yes, but I was thinking of something else. Not about the babies. About us."

She sat down on the other side of the couch with a dazed, hopeless look on her face. "We've got to get these kids to sleep through the night, Steve, or I'm headed for a breakdown. I'm not sure whether it will be my mind or body that goes first."

I was surprised she hadn't reached this point sooner. I'd run five marathons, but I knew nothing of endurance compared to my wife. We decided to hire an infant sleep consultant named Davis Ehrler. She came to our home on the evening of April 23, 2006. That date remains forever etched in my memory, because it's the day that everything changed.

Shelley, her parents, Lauren, and I assembled at our house

to await Davis's arrival. I imagined her coming in like a gunslinger entering a saloon, a short, stocky woman with thick forearms and quick temper. Tumbleweeds would roll by, the piano player would stop, and all of us would freeze in her steely gaze. That's what I imagined. What I got was a tall, slender, blond woman dressed to the nines, who bounded into our house like a cheerleader.

Davis introduced herself to everyone, including the kids, with a warm smile. She made a point of memorizing each child's name and talking to them for a few minutes. Then she went to work. She ditched the cheerleader persona and took command, but more like a confident military officer than drill sergeant. She was firm and direct without being abrupt or forceful.

"When I got here at 6 o'clock, I could tell that your babies were already exhausted," she said. "They were whiny and listless. Like most babies, your kids don't get enough sleep. One-year-olds need twelve hours of sleep at night and two ninety-minute naps a day. Most parents do things to keep their kids from getting enough sleep because they want babies to stop crying. The child cries from fatigue, and the parent responds by doing something that stimulates the child in order to get her to stop crying. They give her a bottle, distract her with a toy, or stick in a Baby Einstein video with the best intentions, unaware that they're only preventing her from falling asleep."

Shelley and I looked at each other, chagrined. We did this kind of stuff all the time.

"So let me get this straight," I said. "Our kids should be sleeping twelve hours a night?"

"Yes," said Davis.

"And this is possible in the material world, not Middle-Earth or some other dimension?"

Davis didn't blink.

"So what's the trick?" I asked. "Is there some special white noise machine you use or something?"

"Absolutely not," she said, eyes wide as if I'd just said a dirty word. "Part of the problem is that parents use too many crutches that prevent their children from learning to sleep. Things like rocking, feeding, electric crib aquariums, and white noise machines help in the short run …"

I gulped. Shelley blushed. We had used all of those things.

" … but prevent the baby from learning something very important—if she lies down and closes her eyes, it will make her feel better."

"But they just keep crying if we don't do those things," said Shelley. "It seems impossible to soothe them without it."

Davis sighed and smiled patiently.

"At a year old, babies usually don't cry in their cribs at bedtime because they're afraid," she explained. "They don't feel abandoned; they feel frustrated. They're in pain from fatigue and don't know what to do about it. You have to give them the chance to figure it out."

I agreed with her on this to a point. I thought kids younger than ten months might genuinely be scared, but kids closer to a year old with good parental attachment were probably just mad that no one was rocking or feeding them. Regardless, understanding that our kids were aggravated rather than afraid made all the difference. It made us willing to put them in their cribs and see what happened.

We gave the kids their last bottle in the living room with

all the lights on. I had Jordan and started rocking him out of habit.

"No rocking, Steve," said Davis.

"Doh!" I said, but she didn't laugh.

When the kids finished their bottles, we kissed them good-night, put them in their cribs, and shut the door. Things were quiet for about ten seconds. Then the sound of Armageddon came from the babies' two bedrooms. There was weeping and wailing and gnashing of teeth. Ella screamed, "Dada!" which was plain old playing dirty. Shelley and I were prepared for hours of this, resigned to a long night of anguish for everybody. We doubted we would get much sleep.

Then something unexpected happened. Something glorious and incredible and thank-you-Jesus-for-saving-our-butts mirac-ulous. After thirty minutes of screaming like banshees, the kids started to settle down. For the next fifteen minutes, we heard sporadic bursts of protest, but the bawling barrage had stopped. Bursts of crying came between longer and longer intervals of silence, like microwave popcorn when it's done cooking. Then, no more than forty-five minutes after we put them in their cribs, everything was quiet. It was 7 p.m.

They slept for thirteen hours.

The next day, they took two ninety-minute naps, crying for about twenty minutes after Shelley put them down. That night, we put them to bed at six and they cried for about thirty minutes … then slept for thirteen hours. The next night, they cried for fifteen minutes … then slept for thirteen hours. The next night they cried for five minutes … then slept for thirteen hours. By Friday night, they did nothing but giggle and coo when we put them in bed. Emma nestled under the covers and shut her eyes as soon as she hit the mattress.

For a year, we'd been rocking babies until ten o'clock, sometimes later. Then they would awake around one, demanding to be fed. During the day, we rocked and bounced and pleaded with them to go down for a nap. Now they took two naps a day and went to bed at six without so much as a snivel.

On Tuesday evening of that week, a mere two days after Davis' visit, Shelley and I sat down to dinner *together*. The meal was cooked on a stove instead of in a microwave. There was a bottle of wine and a flickering candle on the table. Halfway through the meal, I looked up at Shelley and said, "Hi. I'm Steve. Aren't we married or something?"

What happened after that is none of your business.

I hadn't realized how much the constant stress and sleep deprivation had taken a toll. The first week after the kids started sleeping through the night, I made over a dozen different changes at the clinic, fixing problems that I'd been sleepwalking past for a year. I started exercising again. Shelley started walking our fat and fidgety dogs again. She started reading books and watching television at night instead of spending her evenings in a rocking chair. And every night that I didn't have to work late was like a party. I'd get home early, play with the kids for an hour, put them to bed, and then we'd eat dinner. I bought a new grill and started cooking out. We even had friends over for dinner. And they stayed late. And got rowdy sometimes. The babies slept through it all.

The new quality time with Shelley resuscitated our marriage. More importantly, it gave us time to debrief about what we had just been through. We reviewed the past two years, working through the miscarriages, the pregnancy, and the first year of our children's lives. We each listened as the other told us about things we didn't notice because we were so overwhelmed. For the first time, we joked about the things that had made us miserable. We even laughed about our insane fights. We were Steve and Shelley again instead of a couple of snarling parent-things. God had granted our children the grace to sleep. He'd given us Davis to help us do something we couldn't do on our own. Just like it says in Psalm 40, God lifted us out of the slimy pit and set our feet on a rock. Now, we got to look down into the pit and talk about what it had been like to live there for a year. Sometimes, we even did it laughing.

After everything we'd been through, I had started to see life as an endless cycle of suffering-recovery-happiness-repeat. By the time my kids started sleeping through the night, I knew better than to think that the cycle wouldn't start again soon. I figured we were just getting a nice break before the kids became toddlers and started to destroy the house. What I didn't know was that there was a deep, sacred process going on. God was teaching me about a joy that transcends the cycle of pain and pleasure. He was showing me that there is something outside of life's seasons, something other than the rise and fall of fortune. He wanted me to discover the joy that lies outside of happiness and suffering, in something greater than myself. Though I didn't know it during that blissful spring of 2006, God had sent four exceptional teachers to train me in the ways of joy. They lived in my house, but I hadn't really met them yet.

12

Grace
in Sciatica

AS OUR CHILDREN'S FIRST BIRTHDAY APPROACHED AT the beginning of May, Shelley and I were in high spirits. Fears about the babies' health and development had all but vanished. Since they were born prematurely, we'd worried about everything from infection to developmental disorders to cerebral palsy. Seeing our children healthy, happy, and developing rapidly put our minds at ease. Watching them sleep fourteen to sixteen hours a day made things even better.

In the midst of all this, I made the mistake of thinking that life was normal again. I thought I could have my old life back. I thought I could recover everything I'd been denied for the last year. I was going to exercise, write more, and get back to some of the frivolity of my pre-quadruplet life. I'd become this cool, fit dad who managed to be both productive and fun.

A common saying goes, "If you want to give God a laugh, tell him your plans." As I rushed to reclaim my old life, God was laughing so hard that milk was coming out of his nose.

Before the kids came, I was an avid runner. I'd run five marathons and pounded out thirty-five miles a week when I was taking it easy. If I had a race coming up, I'd put in fifty miles, sixty if it was a marathon. This included speed work, interval training, and hill repeats. During the kids' first year, however, I was lucky if I managed to get in ten miles a week at a snail's pace. Once they started sleeping through the night, I assumed that I could bounce back to my previous fitness level in no time. I'd start running races again, and Shelley would be waiting for me at the finish line with my beautiful children. Maybe I'd even get one of those custom quadruplet jogging strollers and run some short races while pushing them in front of me.

I went to the gym to begin my journey back to glory. I was sweating and feeling good. I hadn't worked out this hard in months. It made me feel cocky, like not even a year of quadruplets could impede my fitness. In this fit of hubris, I decided to do an extra set on the lat pull-down machine. My first few reps felt too easy, so I added twenty pounds. I reached up, grabbed the bar, and pulled down with sanguine confidence.

Owww.

A sharp pain radiated from my lower back. I grimaced but decided to work through it. Just a little kink. Another few reps and it would vanish. I pulled down on the bar again.

OWWW!

A voice in my head, possibly Shelley's or my mother's, told me to stop. I ignored it and pulled down again.

This time, I said a lot more than "Ow!"

My back was on fire. I rolled aside and collapsed on the gym floor. A woman rushed over to me, asking if I was okay. I told her I was fine—which was a big, fat lie. It felt like someone was poking my lower back with a cattle prod. Gritting my teeth and trying not to scream, I limped out of the gym and drove home through waves of pain.

I ended up in bed for a week.

A year of sporadic sleep, donated casseroles, and a few thousand hours in a rocking chair had taken their toll. My body wasn't about to tolerate a rapid transition back to youthful vigor. The pain in my lower back progressed down my left leg. Within a week, I couldn't walk without an electric shock shooting from my hip to my toes. I had to take a week off work because I could barely tie my shoes. I looked around the Web for a diagnosis and was incredulous when I found one that matched my symptoms.

"Sciatica?" I shouted. "Only old people get that! No way. This is just a temporary thing."

Three days later, I went to the doctor. He said, "You have sciatica."

I was outraged. Just when I thought I'd gotten my life back, a stupid geriatric disorder ruined everything. I couldn't exercise. I couldn't lift weights, much less anything else over ten pounds. Even walking hurt. Only prescription painkillers helped, but all they did was make me not care that I could barely move. The whole thing felt like a bait-and-switch. Our kids were sleeping through the night, but I couldn't benefit from it because of a problem I'd only heard my grandmother talk about.

"I can't have sciatica, Shelley!" I said. "You know me. I can't sit still for one minute."

"I guess you don't have a choice," she said.

And so I sat.

I sat around chatting with my wife, reading to my kids, and watching television with the whole family. And it was exactly what I needed to do.

Ever since the kids had been born, I had been thanking God they were all healthy; but I'd been too exhausted and overwhelmed to enjoy their vivacious lives. Sciatica gave me the grace to be still, something I'm terrible at. I needed to slow down and enjoy my son and daughters. They needed my new energy. They needed me to be focused and present as they learned to walk and talk, which they did with a vengeance once we were all getting plenty of sleep. They didn't need a dad preoccupied with getting his old life back; they needed a dad who would sit down, shut up, and embrace his new one.

During my bout with sciatica, I began to realize that my new life was so much better than the old one. I slowed down and realized that life felt more complete than it ever had. See, running is a good metaphor for how I lead my life. I chase things. I run after attention, wealth, success, beauty—and pretty much anything that's hard to catch. Ecclesiastes 2:17 calls this "chasing after the wind." But God made me stop running, both literally and figuratively. He wanted me to pay attention to what I had instead of chasing what I didn't. Once I could hardly move because of the sciatica, I started to pay attention to the abundant life God had given me.

A lot of little things woke me up to how much better life was now. The kids started to say "Hi, Dada," in unison when I got home from work. They climbed all over me when picking them up was too painful. One of the kids would walk up to me with one of their little cardboard books and say, "Read book?" Then I'd pull them onto my lap and read to them. Ella started giving me kisses. Hayley started giving me hugs. Emma tickled me and put together puzzles with me. Jordan would tackle me in a bear hug. How could I not love being the father of four? How on earth could I think that training for a 10K was better? Even though I was in my worst physical shape in years and I'd gained twenty pounds, it didn't send me into a panic like it once would have. Even though I wasn't meeting my writing goals and the ascent of my career had tapered, I didn't care. We had all four of our children at the same time. There had been no waiting between bundles of joy. A year before, that had seemed frightening and unjust. Now, I couldn't imagine it any other way.

As I was leaving for work one morning, I saw Jordan watching me. He'd climbed up on the couch and was looking at me through our front window. By now, he understood what it meant when I got in my car carrying my briefcase. He started crying and banging on the window. Through the glass I could hear him shouting, "Dada! Dada!" Tears were streaming down his face. I couldn't stand it. I went back in the house and captured him in a hug. I made funny noises until he started laughing. Then I got him involved in something else so I could slip out the door. Once I was in my car and down the street, it was my turn to cry.

That moment, just like the sciatica, was painful. But it was a lesson that I needed. I'll need it again and again and again until I get it through my thick skull that I already have an abundant life. God will have to beat me about the head and shoulders on a regular basis until I stop chasing shadows and phantoms. There's a part of me that refuses to accept that I don't need more. I never feel smart enough, fit enough, or wealthy enough. It's hard for me to believe that there's not more fun to be had around the next corner. The good news is that it doesn't take as much as it used to for me to see that this isn't true. Now, all it takes is one of my children crying because I'm leaving. They know I'll be back, but they don't even like it when I'm gone for a little while. How much more do I need to convince me that

I'm worth something? Why do I think that there's some rush or high that's better than the love of my family?

However, I think God understands that it's hard for me to trust the steady joy he's given me. Occasionally, he gift-wraps joy in something stimulating enough to get my attention. He uses pain if he has to, but I think he prefers to use fun. I usually frolic and conjure merriment as a diversion from boredom and stress, but, once in a while, God gives me a real reason to party.

Like our kids' first birthday.

Few things in life thrill me more than throwing a party. When I'm hosting a festive event, even the details for planning it seem fun. I turn into some sort of frat-boy mutation of Martha Stewart. I make sure everything is clean and tidy. I get anything anyone might possibly need and a lot of things that they don't. I obsess over the music, trying to pick something for everybody and organizing the playlist for maximum fun.

For our kids' first birthday, we pulled out all the stops. We hired a caterer. We rented tables with umbrellas. We had more varieties of food and beverage than a Las Vegas buffet. We spent way too much money but didn't care—because this was an important celebration.

In addition to celebrating our children, we were thanking the people who had made it all possible. On the day of the party, almost a hundred people squeezed into our tiny backyard. We invited all the family, friends, neighbors, clergy, church members, doctors, and nurses who helped us survive. We told them not to bring presents (though most of them ignored us). We wanted to shower them with thanks and love. The people packing our backyard that day had shown me that joy is never an individual thing.

That day, it was easy for me to embrace joy. I frolicked and laughed and ran around like an idiot. I tossed my children in the air, then let our guests pass them around.

"Daddy funny!" Hayley explained to Ryan as I put her in his arms for the first time.

"Sweetie," he said, "you have no idea. He'd better hope I don't start telling stories about just how funny he is."

"Do you want me to get you a drink or pour one on you, chump?" I said, and he laughed.

I made sure all my kids were okay and having fun. Then I started playing host.

"What can I get for you?" I asked Margie, the fearless leader of our volunteers. "Something to eat, something to drink?"

"What's gotten into you?" she said. "For a man who has back problems, you sure seem happy."

I laughed, but deep down inside I was holding onto something delicate, holy. When I let down my guard and stop acting like the rest of the world is in my way, God can show others love through me. When I let go of cynicism and surrender to the assault of joy, the divine flows through me.

If you were going to pick two words to describe a typical day with one year-old quadruplets, they would probably be *loudness* and *motion*. I love that stuff. I like creating it. I like using it to help my children experience joy. In a family with quadruplets, maybe it's good to have a dad who loves throwing a party.

Maybe God picked the right guy, after all.

13

Quadruplets in Color

I'M BEING ACCOSTED BY JOY. THE BABIES ARE CRAWLING all over me, and I can't stop laughing. Just then Shelley walks in. Oops—I forgot I was supposed to have diapers changed and clothes on before I left for work. But I'd been having too much fun to think about such mundane tasks.

"Um ... I haven't had time," I said. "Things have been crazy."

"Yeah, right," she said. Hayley thought this was funny and started laughing.

I gave everyone a hug, got off the floor, and started dressing the kids. We talked and laughed and hugged. I could see that my kids loved me. Even their tantrums usually resulted from wanting attention while I was busy dressing someone else. There was nothing subtle about their affection. It poured out, uninhibited by fear or shame. It drew out a deep, potent love in me that I'd been afraid to show.

Shelley brought them up to the clinic one afternoon, and everyone at work got to observe me with my children. I was so excited to see them in the middle of the workday that I forgot that over a dozen of my students were watching me.

I picked up Jordan and tossed him in the air. A longtime student and friend named Bryan said, "Toss him here!" I hurled Jordan through the air to Bryan. Shelley furrowed her brow at me, but Jordan laughed so hard that his face turned red.

Then Emma was upset about something. My brain had become hardwired to respond to the sound of a crying baby, and I dashed over. I started making funny faces until she laughed. Hayley and Ella started laughing when they saw me. Never one to pass up an attentive audience, I started making sounds like a monkey. It never occurred to me that the students were looking on as their professor behaved like a drunken caveman.

Finally, they had to go home and I made it a point to kiss everyone good-bye. After they were gone, one of my students said, "Who was that guy in here with your kids? He looked like you, but he didn't act anything like you. He was a big sweetie."

Someone else said, "It was nice to see a softer side of you. I didn't know that was there until I saw you with your children."

I knew it was there. I was just afraid to show it. But my kids are teaching me not to be afraid. They love it when I express loud, raucous affection. They eat it up when I shower them with kisses and hugs. They're thrilled when I act goofy. Their faces light up when I tell them how wonderful they are and how much I love them.

I know it won't always be that way. When they hit eleven or twelve, they might roll their eyes and grimace when I pile on the love. But I won't give them a hard time, and I'll give them their space. I owe it to them. I learn more from them than they will ever learn from me. When they laugh so hard they can't open their eyes and their bellies shake. When some new wonder makes them oblivious to all else. When being tossed up in the air and spun around means more than all the riches in the world, I get a glimpse of what matters most. At long last, I am learning about joy.

. . .

God uses the ebb and flow of suffering and happiness to teach us things. I still believe that. I think God teaches us about our strengths and gifts through struggles. I think he teaches us gratitude and peace during the happy times. But I think joy stands outside the process altogether. Something bigger than suffering or happiness calls us. We need more than a mission statement and goals that match our gifts. Amidst all our striving, we need the quiet, steady peace that comes from being attached to something other than our own fortunes. Joy comes from being attached to something other than yourself. *Someone*, actually.

A lot of things in creation model this attachment. For some people, joy comes from being devoted to a cause. It can come from work and creativity. But I think it mostly comes through relationships. It comes from bonds that last through the good times and the bad. It's the feeling that, no matter what happens, we will be connected to another. I think that's what joy is.

I became a cynic because I didn't believe in the power of that connection. I thought suffering destroyed that connection. I thought confusion or pain meant God had turned his back on me.

Through my family, God is knocking the cynicism out of me. That's what happens when you love others so much that you'd give up your very last Red Bull for them. The freefall between pain and pleasure still confounds me, and I wish it would stop. But love doesn't go away, especially God's love. That's what matters. This kind of love is outside of karma and the winds of change. It's what brings me joy.

The
Still Point

THIS STORY ISN'T ABOUT FINDING AN ENDING BUT discovering a new beginning. Our children are two years old now. As I write this, I can hear them outside playing with Shelley and her parents. (I'm inside waiting for a pizza to arrive.) It's hard to believe that not long ago, we were worried about their survival. We were afraid that something would be wrong if they did survive. Now, I can hear our dog Bella barking, probably because one of the kids is chasing her. I hear Hayley shouting, "No!" I hear Ella talking in long, rambling sentences to her grandmother. I hear Jordan shouting, "Fan!" because the air conditioning compressor just switched on. I hear Emma giggling and squealing with delight. I hear the sounds of joy.

As our kids have gotten older, things have gotten easier—and harder. It's easier because they're not as helpless anymore. That's also the reason that things are harder. We've cordoned off our valuables in one section of the living room, because you don't want fragile objects within reach of our children. They're learning about jumping and climbing, which is a lot of fun until one them goes, as they would say, "Kaboom!" They've learned about using violence to settle disputes and whining to get what they want. We've had to start setting limits and giving time outs. But it's a small price to pay. Their episodes of defiance are brief and merely evidence that they're becoming little people. Other than the occasional spat or tantrum, our kids have delightful personalities.

Hayley remains the comedian. Not only does she still laugh at everything, but also she's learned how to make everyone else laugh. This makes giving her time outs difficult, because she knows exactly how to crack me up when I'm supposed to be punishing her. Ella talks so much that she seems years older. After we put her to bed, she babbles with her sisters like she's a teenager on a cell phone. Jordan is more of a truck than ever, but he's proving that he's got brains to go with the brawn. He knows the names of all the planets, and he can point out different parts of a truck, including the grill and the exhaust pipe. Emma is still a little scientist, but she's become the most affectionate. She loves hugging her sisters and cuddling with her parents. Every couple of weeks, somebody does something new and wonderful. As much as work as our kids are, they're the source of endless delight and surprises.

Shelley is still tired and overworked, but her spirits are higher than ever. Being the mother of quadruplets has become her passion and calling. It's so clear that she's the perfect mother for these children. Her heart is a bottomless wellspring of love. She showers our children with attention and affection, even when she's exhausted and overwhelmed. I'll watch her struggle to get out of bed, but then hear her giggling and showering our children with praise seconds after she's left the bedroom. Her training as a psychologist has also been invaluable. She's turned mothering multiples into a science. She does research, collects data, and tests different methods until she devises the perfect solution for our latest problem. I have no doubt that her talents will someday help other families with multiples. I might write stories about our kids, but Shelley will someday write a manual for parents of multiples.

Our marriage is hanging in there too. Shelley and I are figuring out new ways to be husband and wife instead of just parents all the time. We get more quality time together. We're having more fun. She's eager to support my work away from home, and I'm learning to take her lead around the house. I'm more likely to say, "Okay" or "Sorry," instead of exhaling loudly and shouting, "Unbelievable!"

The truth is that I'm still trying to get over all the same hurdles. I'm still impatient. I'm still selfish. I get bored too easily and I forget things. I still show affection through sarcasm when just being nice would work a lot better. But I'm not as much of a cynic anymore. God's surrounded me with too much joy. There's a vibration of peace beneath the noise and struggle. In the poem "Burnt Norton," T. S. Eliot calls this quiet joy "the still point." In describing a kingfisher jumping out of the water, Eliot writes,

> *the light is still*
> *At the still point of the turning world.*

For Eliot, the ebb and flow of pain and pleasure revolves around a still point. That's where joy exists. It's where God resides. Our lives revolve around it. We will suffer. We will enjoy. We will succeed. We will fail. We will celebrate, and we will mourn. We will love, and our hearts will be broken. The cycle won't end until Christ perfects us in eternity. Psalm 46:10 says, "Be still, and know that I am God." In the midst of all our striving and restlessness, we must look for Christ. If we can do that, we'll know joy.

T. S. Eliot finishes "Burnt Norton" with a stanza that begins with these lines:

> *There rises the hidden laughter*
> *Of children in the foliage....*

As I'm writing this, I hear the laughter of my children outside. That sound makes my other worries seem ridiculous. It makes me seem ridiculous. My past and future become small in comparison. My children expose my cynicism as nothing but a sad waste. They reveal the hidden laughter of God, calling me to seek him at the still point of the turning world.

Acknowledgments

HAVING QUADRUPLETS HAS TAUGHT ME THAT WE DON'T really accomplish anything without the grace and support of others.

Angela Scheff saw the book I wanted to write before I did and lent her wisdom to its writing.

Shelley Showalter, Rebecca Brown, and Sandi Rog provided invaluable feedback that made this a better book.

Vickie and Todd Showalter created time and space for me to write by giving their time, energy, and love to our children.

Without the people of St. Luke's of the Mountains, I'd probably be in an institution instead of writing books about joy.

And without Shelley, Hayley, Ella, Jordan, and Emma, this book wouldn't exist.